OPPOR

KNOCKING

How to Open the Door to Rental Property Investment and Management

PAUL W. JAMISON SR.

REAL ESTATE BROKER & INVESTOR

SPARK Publications
Charlotte, North Carolina

Opportunity Is Knocking: How to Open the Door to Rental Property Investment and Management
Paul W. Jamison Sr.

Designed, produced, and published by SPARK Publications
SPARKpublications.com
Charlotte, NC

Printed in the United States
Softcover, September 2019, ISBN: 978-1-943070-59-6
Library of Congress Control Number: 2019911582

DEDICATION

This book is dedicated to my mentor, Bill Jamison, also known as Dad, Pappaw, and Grandpa. He has been the spark in my interest and love of real estate. Throughout his life, he set an example of determination to overcome obstacles and evaluate life and decisions through rational thinking and doing the hard work. He showed me that financial prosperity is possible in many ways, but most certainly real estate can and always will be one of the best.

Table of Contents

THE JOURNEY 1

CHAPTER 1 | Know Your Why 13

CHAPTER 2 | Communicate Effectively.................... 39

CHAPTER 3 | Identify Your Investment Property 49

CHAPTER 4 | Get the Property Rent-Ready.......................... 61

CHAPTER 5 | Establish the Rent..73

CHAPTER 6 | Write the Lease... 85

CHAPTER 7 | Screen Tenants 99

CHAPTER 8 | Move Them In 119

CHAPTER 9 | Account for the Money....................................129

CHAPTER 10 | Perform Inspections..................................... 141

CHAPTER 11 | Manage Repairs 153

CHAPTER 12 | Move Them Out 171

CHAPTER 13 | Evict Them...179

CHAPTER 14 | Use a Property Management Company.......189

CHAPTER 15 | Vacation for Fun and Profit 199

APPENDIX | Downloadable Resources 221

ABOUT THE AUTHOR 233

THE JOURNEY

I can't really remember how long ago I fell in love with investment real estate. I can only guess it goes back to 1983 when my father and I purchased a triplex in Cincinnati, Ohio. I lived on the main floor and had tenants on the second and third floors. It was the greatest thing. Every month, I put two rent checks in the bank along with the amount my father and I agreed on to pay down the mortgage. I knew once the mortgage was paid off, those rent checks would supplement my income. I could buy another property or maybe just a fancy car.

At that time in my life, money had a different meaning. As the father of two small boys, I couldn't hold onto it for long. But it did keep coming. That part left an impression.

Moving to the Carolinas put the next stage of investment on hold. In order for my wife, Kerry, and me to buy our first house together, we needed the money from the triplex for a down payment. Our business was just getting off the ground in Charlotte, and every spare dollar we had was invested back into the business.

Like any passion, even when the money wasn't there, we still kept looking for real estate. Everywhere I went, I looked, poked, checked out vacation rentals, and researched options for someone else to provide a retreat for us to enjoy when time allowed. I even bought the Carlton Sheets series of tapes and workbooks to learn how "someone else" could finance my vision or how I could use "someone else's money" to make my mailbox-money dreams come true.

At the time (around the mid to late '90s) due to my schedule and the rapid growth of our business, I owned and piloted an airplane.

We would fly from Charlotte to Cincinnati and to Siesta Key, Florida, where the market was really hot. Man, was that exciting. We would fly down and meet with a Realtor® to view properties. Our first property was an ocean-view condo on Siesta Key across from the public beach. From there the momentum began. Kerry and my mother-in law, Kathy, would go to the store, buy every stitch of furniture my credit card would hold, and decorate a gorgeous unit that would make anyone want to stay there. Let the rental world begin!

The School of Hard Knocks

Siesta Key was a great learning experience. We ended up buying a total of five units there and a model home in Bradenton that we leased back to the builder. Over three years, we bought, sold, and rented them all. The very last one I purchased was the crème de la crème—the penthouse suite. I bought it without even seeing it for $1.2 million. I trusted the Realtor® and had made a great deal of money—and he was making a stinkin' killing. At that point, I didn't know what I didn't know, and the learning officially began. My Realtor® had a "partner" who was also the mortgage officer. I later found out that combination was a true double-edged sword. I wonder now why I did not ask more questions.

As long as the units were renting and properties were moving around, the journey was great, even with the cost of being an out-of-state owner. They absolutely pummel you if you are not a full-time resident. On the penthouse alone, I was paying $28,000 in taxes and homeowners' association (HOA) fees annually. That didn't include the mortgage and was before a renter stepped foot in the unit. Then came the management company fees, the income tax, the assessments to do this or that, and so on. After years of therapy … just kidding. Seriously though, this was a 1,100-square-foot, top-floor condo with a gorgeous view, but what I really owned was air. In most condos, you only own the air inside the walls, not the building. I mean, are you kidding me? Air should never (nor will I ever again allow it to) cost me that much. But I was making money—or at least it felt like it.

Around the same time in Charlotte, a business partner and I bought a 10,000-square-foot historic building near uptown Charlotte to run our ad agency. It took us a long time to complete the renovations. In the area at the time, if you looked outside, shopping carts pushed around the block by homeless people were the most common form of four-wheel transportation. But we saw a rosy road ahead, and with our Fortune 500 clients doing well, so were we.

The rental properties in Florida and the commercial building in Charlotte, once paid off, would provide ample retirement income and could support us during the next downward trend in the market, which surely would come again in my lifetime (remember back to the triplex where it started). But hey, it wasn't coming soon, so no worries. I kept borrowing, kept buying, and kept going. Leverage was easy. I just called the bank and let them know the amount I needed, and magically the money was there. I got the fancy car too. And the fancy house. And a newer airplane.

Things seemed to click along nicely. My plan was in place, and buying and selling Florida property intentionally slowed down. Kerry and I really only had two properties left down there—the 1,100-square-foot penthouse and the model home. The builder's lease would be up soon, and then we would lease or sell it. The penthouse was renting out for about $65,000 a year gross before management fees, the mortgage, assessments, HOA fees, and taxes. (Translation: a bunch of money tied up for not much in return, and yes, still for owning just air.) But think about those times. You could buy a property in Florida and sell it six months later for $75,000 to $100,000 profit. My Realtor® was working both sides, and I watched him make tremendous money off of me using my money to do it.

In the process, I was learning so much about how it all worked and asking a ton of questions.

I eventually decided to get my real estate license. After more than twenty-five years in the advertising business, I was ready for a change. Off to school I went. I studied furiously and passed the exam the first time, which only about 60 percent of people do.

In order to control the next chapter of my life, I bought out my advertising business partner but kept the business going on a smaller scale. The Carolinas were still on the move, and business was strong. It was easy to just coast during that period. Kerry and I purchased a single rental property near where we lived and rented it out pretty quickly. We were making plans to keep things a bit closer to home.

Then I got a great phone call. Someone was interested in my building uptown. The timing could not have been better. A new stadium had been built a few years back. I could write a whole book on how to hock game-day parking near the stadium. Heck, I used to have Kerry batting her eyelashes and my ten-year-old son, Alex, just looking cute while they yelled at cars to park in our lot. Anyway, a large agency offered me $2.3 million for the building, and that set the stage for some great liquidity. I remember the day it closed. I kept calling the bank to listen to the bank balance on the automated phone line. I had never made that much money at one time in my life. I couldn't wait to spend it on more property. Once I had my real estate license, the whole world had just opened up, and I was an official insider.

We didn't waste any time. The first thing Kerry and I did was purchase a few historic properties. We chose one as our new office. As the oldest building in the town of Matthews, North Carolina, everyone had their eye on it and, of course, their hand in my wallet, including the historic landmark commission. It was in a state of disrepair and needed outer support walls and much of the foundation rebuilt. We spared no expense; from furniture to finishes, we went all the way. I remember finding tin presses to make ceiling tiles to match the era and provide charm. We even found high-tank toilets where you pull the chain to flush.

A house built in 1877 does not have the most-friendly crawl spaces, but it did have some surprises. One day, I found three men on the side of the house huddled together betting money. I asked what the heck they were doing. They grinned toothlessly at me and said they were betting on the number of dead cats we would be bringing out of the crawl space. I could not believe it—why in the heck would they do that? Three hours later, I understood why. To my surprise, thirteen dead, feral cats lay like a crime scene in the back yard. So much for my preconceived notions of dreamy renovations. Not only did we face a feline crime scene, but also my wallet laid down and died right next to those cats. Whatever you think you will spend on an old house, just go ahead and double it for good measure.

When the Bubble Burst

In 2007, after semiretiring from advertising, I began the journey toward a full-time real estate career. Having had my license for a couple years, I was quickly learning and using the proceeds from the uptown building sale to buy real estate. My office, of course, was the first acquisition. I bought lots, land, and houses. At the advice of my financial planner at the time, I leveraged my house, and after I paid for a piece of property, I then leveraged it to continue to buy more. I put it all out there. I wanted the rental income. I wanted to develop the land. I wanted to become a large real estate player in the market.

My property management prowess at this point was just on my own properties, self-managing and having my bookkeeper run the financials on QuickBooks. I knew to keep the security deposits separate and began to assemble properties. My Florida experience was coming to a close, almost. I still had the penthouse, which was still performing about the same, and the bills kept coming.

The model home lease would be ending soon; both Florida properties had a mortgage and HOAs that were hungry since people began defaulting.

It was an awesome year. I started my real estate agency, hired a few support folks, built up to fourteen agents, rented my properties, and had the land assemblage under contract to a Christian sports organization for over $2 million. Yes, I was leveraged to the hilt. I had ten rentals in town (ranches, I am a ranch house guy), one in Florida, plus land and two historic buildings. Debt was significant. (I am embarrassed to say exactly how much.) Liquidity was fair, rents could make the payments, and my agents were selling houses.

Then it started. It felt like everything changed overnight. I never expected it, never wanted to see it. Before I knew what happened, the real estate business just stopped. It quit, kaput, *DONE.* My volume just hit the skids. I remember getting a call from the bank—it was going out of business and called my note for $700,000. The Christian sports buyer for my land bailed out on me and stuck me with a $44,000 refund of the hard deposit. My lender on my office building called and said my ratios were no longer in compliance, raised my interest rate, and put me in "special assets." I had never missed a payment, never been late. I had some liquidity but was not sure it was enough to make it through what sounded like a terrible hole ahead.

I couldn't see how it happened until someone shined a light in the hole I had dug for myself. Credit was so easy—just fog a mirror, and you can buy it. Truth: I should have known. It was my fault. I can remember my father's voice telling me, "Son, you will always make good decisions when times are bad and bad decisions when times are good."

The journey to better investment property and theory began here. The journey to property management began here. The decisions to change my investment philosophy and debt philosophy changed here. It all changed here. When we had to move out of Kerry's dream house to rent it, we moved into a ranch rental next to a transient apartment complex next to the train tracks. To top if off, an angry train conductor blew his whistle nonstop as he came through town at 2 a.m. We often wonder to this day who was the person that upset this guy. When I had to sell the airplane and leave the private club, it was a lonely time. I was determined to make it different. And the journey to that change is why I am writing this book.

Learning from Mistakes

Kerry and I knew that God had a path for us, and we needed to look outside ourselves. With His help and a ton of hard work we were able to overcome. In Philippians, the apostle Paul talks about the things of this world and the things that matter. It's hard to keep those perspectives, especially when things stink.

When the recession hit, we had choices to make. We needed to change our business and our mindset. Thankfully, our ten income-producing properties were able to generate their debt load in income even though the bank owned a piece of many of them (the mortgage). This stuck with me. I remember thinking that many people were looking to rent because times were not as fruitful, so if I couldn't sell them a house, surely I could rent them one. I kept them happy, and they kept paying.

I sold the Florida condo at a $200,000 loss and the model home at break even. But at least that pain was over. I could focus on a more localized strategy and keep things where I could easily keep my eyes and hands on them.

As I mentioned earlier, we'd moved out of Kerry's dream house and rented it out. We also moved the real estate agency out of the historic property and into a retail environment next to a coffee shop for exposure. An attorney—they always seem to have money— rented the historic building from us. We still had a receptionist and a few agents. All the rest had either moved on or left the business.

To be focused on the sales side of my business, I decided first that I needed help with managing my properties. In 2009, I handed over one of my rentals on a trial basis to a local property management company. My hope was to get to a place where I could hand over all my rentals to them and focus my strategy on the retail or house sales side of my business.

Needless to say, my property management experience stunk with the company I chose. If after reading this book you decide to hire a management company, ask a ton of questions. (Sound familiar?) It really is not a simple business, but it does have the right name. "Property management" means they should manage the property. But I ended up finding the renter, handling the maintenance, and taking all the tenant's calls. On top of that, I had to wait till the end of the month to get my money. That was definitely not how it should be done.

After twenty-seven years of running an advertising agency and helping clients grow, it became time to take my own advice. I entered real estate full time and faced a down market in a crowded field. First step, I launched a radio strategy on WBT, a local talk-radio station, with a weekly show that cost me $1,000 a week. People said I was nuts. But in advertising, we constantly told our clients to spend money when no one is spending it and where no one is spending it. So that's what I did. I created a show to educate people on real estate. We brought on guests, talked, and even later started going live to take callers. The preparation for the one-hour show forced me to educate myself about the market, its conditions, its opportunities, and get a pulse on what people wanted, needed, and would do. I knew it could take at least a year to see results.

So there I was: making changes and corrections but still leveraged to the hilt. A personal loan from a friend came in at just the right time. It worked well for both of us. He had some real estate as collateral and a better interest rate than the banks were paying, and I had an interest-only loan to carry me through that time. What a blessing.

As soon as the one year was up with that property management company, I fired them. And this is where the story takes a turn. I was openly sharing my frustration with my dear friend Marissa. She listened intently and shared her own challenge of finding a good property management solution for a client of hers. After much discussion, she chimed in with her bold fashion, "Jamison, you are managing all your properties by yourself already. You'd think you'd be good at it by now. Why don't you manage a couple for me?" After thinking about it, I agreed.

Little did I know that her client was in the midst of building a real estate fund, and a year later I would be in charge of a local office for them in North and South Carolina managing several hundred rental properties. I remember going to the courthouse for them with $1.5 million in blank certified checks to bid on properties at the courthouse steps in Georgia. We would bid on, buy, and then rent out properties like a well-oiled machine. Separately, I managed seventy properties for individual owners. I never dreamed I would find myself in that position. It provided a small salary, medical benefits, and the freedom to recover. The path presented itself, and I worked seven days a week, dawn till dusk.

I ran my real estate brokerage and managed the real estate fund's properties along with my individual property owners who could not sell because of the economic climate and who became what were affectionately called "incidental investors." Some, of course, were intentional, but many had no other option in that economy. I remember sitting in front of a prospect, as I had so many times before, who could not sell their house because of the market or because they simply owed more than the home was worth. They would ask me how in the world I could protect them from renters who always tear up the house, leave them without rent, and make their family home a shamble worthy of being torn down. I heard it so many times—that same notion of the terrible tenant on a path of destruction. Everyone knew someone who had that happen.

I learned firsthand from managing my own property the value of what is expected. I understand what it's like to be on the edge of financial ruin. I understand why this business will never be perfect and why it will never be fully predictable. We humans are not predictable. Life is just not that way. I learn every day. I make mistakes regularly—it's what you do with those mistakes and what you apply from them that matters. I know the kind of company I do not want to have. I learned that early, and it helped me form the set of principals I follow today in my business.

My investment philosophy is not for everyone. There are many ways to invest. I am not anti-stock market or anti-alternative investment or even anti-leverage. In many ways, I am pro-leverage in some instances. But I am also very clear on what has worked and the type of houses that are consistent. If you really think about the rental market in the right light, when economic times are bad, the rental market does very well. Depending on when you are reading this, the rental market may still do well when times are good. The next generation, and surprisingly even the silver generation, has not expressed a desire to always own their homes, and new levels of tenants are coming into the market all the time.

Buying investment property is not as emotional as buying your family home. But that doesn't mean I don't take it personally when something goes wrong. Someone once told me, "Paul, business is business. Don't take it personally." When someone says that, they are getting ready to screw you over. Make no mistake about it.

I have learned that the property management business is truly codependent. Your investment is nothing without the renter, and the renter is nothing without your rental house. Things happen, and you try to prepare on both sides for those things, but overall, I can't think of any better business of investment to be involved in. I love when my clients that sell reinvest the profit to move the gain forward. I love when clients allow us to handle things for them and preserve the tenant over the long term. It is awesome when it works and requires patience when it doesn't. But as I say in my seminars, a real estate investment will never be worth zero—you can burn it down, blow it up, or trash it, but it's never worth nothing.

As I am writing this book, Jamison Property Management manages just under 400 homes in North Carolina and South Carolina for private investors, and Petra Property Management (in which I am a partner) manages approximately 200 in South Carolina. My wife and I own and operate several million in real estate investment property of our own. (And for the record, I don't buy air any more). Our generous friend is completely paid off, and we are on a journey to purchase more properties and use that revenue to reduce leverage.

We work with many levels of investors and help them build wealth through real estate. In 2018, we handled approximately 170 buyer and seller transactions through our real estate team, many of them to investors. Many of the properties I bought in 2007, I am now turning over for newer and higher returns. At the end of the day, like anything, it's a tool—a tool to help you hedge against stocks, live a life worth living, and give away some money along the way to worthy causes.

We work hard, we evolve, and we get it *DONE*. May you find that same success from this book. My hope is that your journey becomes easier and prosperous by reading these pages. I know there is much more to say, but this gets you down the path. Let's find some great properties together and use my journey to make you some mailbox money.

So why do I do this again?

Why do I rent this house?

CHAPTER 1

Know Your Why

What would possess anybody to buy a piece of property, put a tenant in it whom they probably don't know, and then let them stay there night after night cooking, burning bacon, spilling drinks, and watching TV? I mean, it's like letting strangers throw parties in your house all the time.

As I am writing this chapter, my family and I are staying at one of our rental homes at the coast. I am sitting in a rocking chair enjoying a light breeze, warm sunshine, and an ocean view—but that is now. About an hour and a half ago, it was breakfast time. We bought "real bacon," and my twenty-five-year-old son who lives with us (aaaagh) decided to help get breakfast ready since he rolled out of bed around 10 a.m. (double aaaagh). But at least he wasn't parked on the couch complaining of his hunger.

The bacon was frozen, so first it needed a good thaw. Not a problem—the microwave's defrost setting was pretty self-explanatory. And rather than cook the bacon in a pan, a microwavable dish with paper towels wins the day every time. Six minutes on high tick by. It wasn't done. Another six minutes tick by while he's looking down at his phone for the latest "whatever." He didn't notice the bacon had turned to coal, and the "microwavable" dish was split in two. The house smelled awful.

Believe it or not, we then moved on to phase two of the bacon-cooking challenge. "Let's do it 'the right way' in the pan." *Oh, no.*

You can guess what happened next. The smoke detectors worked (yay). We needed a new pan, so a trip to Walmart was in order. And our house will forever smell of burned bacon. If I know better and still leave a bacon blemish, what are the odds the dozens of families who vacation here will leave marks of their own (that I now own)? (A little play on words. Did you see what I just did there?) So why do I do this again? Why do I rent this house?

For me, real estate investment satisfies many different facets of my personality and goals. Many other people I know do it for completely different areas of opportunity or desire. And a few of those reasons really surprised me. I don't really know what would've happened if I'd started earlier in my life and been more consistent, or if I had listened to my instincts and bought in areas that were a bit more stable. I can't speculate on that. But what I do know is that knowing why you want to invest in real estate will help you understand *who, what, when, where, and how* to have success doing it. Following are some *whys* I've come across in my experience.

Hedging against the Stock Market

This one has been a real eye opener to some of the folks I talk to. It is not an anti-financial product mindset. If you are of any age and have a retirement plan or portfolio of investments, if you don't handle it on your own, you probably have an advisor. I have always said that everyone needs a board of advisors—an investment advisor, an attorney, and a certified public accountant (CPA), and since my wife is reading this, also your spouse.

This team of people together make up your board of advisors. They need to meet together with you at least once a year and make sure you are aligned. Nothing worse than them not rowing with you in the same direction. Have them look at your asset and liability mix and goals and make sure everyone is on the same page. I try to take them out to eat since it is usually cheaper than paying their hourly rate. Or I negotiate a meeting without a fee one or two times a year for this purpose.

Many investment advisors understand the value of having real estate in the portfolio, and many do not. Some fee-based advisors worry about themselves, but I have found them to be the exception. Most understand that diversity of your assets and monthly returns reinvested makes your net worth larger and their accounts larger over time.

The stock market can feel like a roller-coaster ride, and the older I get, the less I want to be on that ride. Roller coasters make me sick in more ways than one. But I understand that life requires balance in almost all things, so here is the point I really want you to get: you actually need a varied investment portfolio strategy. And the stock market's volatility plays a very positive role when it comes to the rental market. Investment property offers a level of control you do not get with stocks, bonds, or mutual funds. You can decide to fix/not fix, change/not change, sell/not sell, and can be in control of your destiny to a higher degree. Does real estate have market volatility like financial products do? Sure, but as I mentioned earlier, it's never worth zero (unless you leverage it to the hilt and have no equity left).

The financial markets make trends a part of their model, and so does real estate. They say about every eight years you will see a downturn. We are well beyond that as I am writing, but I know at some point it's going to come. I see it as an opportunity on two sides. First, it's a buying opportunity. When the market is beat up and you have cash, you can buy while prices are down. Second, believe it or not, when the market is in a downturn, rents are usually on the rise as the number of renters in the market is significantly increased due to conditions in the job market and credit tightening.

On the other hand, when times are good and inventory is short, we see a great trend upward in rent as well. Rents are on the rise even when financial markets are booming due to migration for jobs and lack of inventory. And some folks want to rent in an area for a while before they decide to buy.

Saving for College

When I talked to the investor who came forward to use real estate to save for college, it was a completely new notion to me, but his rationale made perfect sense. He stated that everyone saves and saves for college. Instead, he wanted to buy a rental home for each of his children. *Hmmm,* I thought, *buy a rental home for a child and when they turn eighteen you can get them out of the house and have a place for them to stay.* Then he woke me from my dream. The plan here is to set aside funds—perhaps money from grandparents or other savings you may designate—to purchase a rental home either with or without leverage.

Let's just say for our example that you are using leverage to purchase the home. If you purchase the home and rent it, and the rental amount just covers the mortgage, you are on the right path. If you have excess at times, you can either put it toward principal or self-amortize the payments, meaning to pay more in advance to reduce principal of what you owe faster. Many families put the houses on a fifteen-year mortgage. I, on the other hand, suggest staying with a thirty-year mortgage because somewhere along the way, you will need to buy something for the home or will have a vacancy or may need to make updates. You can always pay like you are on a fifteen-year mortgage or make an extra payment every year to accommodate for vacancy or needed repairs if you need to use some of the cash. But basically, in my client's case, each home was either held by them, the child, or in an

LLC. Please consult your board of advisors (attorney, CPA, financial planner, and/or spouse) for the right thing to do for you.

The ultimate goal is to use the cash flow from the rental home or sale of the rental home to fund college. Many investors of this type take a very direct approach. They use the cash flow from the home to assist with the child's college loan or cost. Then when the child graduates or reaches age thirty, the parent gives the child the home. All that time though, the proceeds were being used to pay down college loans or put a dent into advanced degree costs.

I think this is brilliant. I am not saying or inferring you have to hand the child the house either. But as you will see from my philosophy, you may want to sell and rebuy using proceeds in a tax-free exchange (more on that later) if that meets your plan, but eventually it too can be used for your retirement. It's kind of like the gift that keeps on giving. It does cost you along the way, but under the right scenario, it also can keep giving all the way through you or your child's life.

Who knows? They may want to live there after college. So many options here—pick one that is right for you. Today the average student leaves college with a debt load of $360 per month. That is only going to continue to go up. Why not let someone else (a renter) pay for your child's education? And control the money without the market volatility that some riskier accounts can have.

Estate Planning

Your board of advisors will definitely play a large role if this is your *why*. It is one of the mechanisms I personally plan to use to pass wealth on to my children. I do not plan to just drop money or an insurance policy on them. I plan to provide them with a tool to manage wealth well into their future if they so choose. I think about that not just for my children but also for my wife if I am to pass before her. I want a good, sheltered way to provide her with a monthly income she can control moving forward. Also, one of my children may need some additional help along the way in his life, and at a minimum, my investment property could provide a place for him to live without the cost of a mortgage or burden of debt.

Planning is crucial. Consult with your board of advisors on how best to hold assets and how to transfer them to your spouse or children. You can set rules around those assets and how they are sold and even how your children have to handle the assets after you pass. I have provisions in my trust for the grandchildren and, heaven forbid, provisions in the unhappy case of divorce or death of my children. It is a blessing to be able to pass on the fruits of your labor to your children. It is even more of a blessing to know that if you pass, you are able to make sure your spouse has the monthly income he or she will need to live a good, solid life without you.

Being selfish here, I also like having that income so that I won't be a burden on my kids as I age or cause a rift in the family around living with them. Rental income cash flow can allow you to stay in your home with a caregiver. Don't get me wrong—I love my kids. But based on where I want to be and the strong desire I have to be independent, I want them to live their own lives and come visit once in a while. As I've said time and again, I want to live in a house small enough where my kids constantly know they are welcome, just not to move in.

Even if estate planning isn't your primary why, it's still important for any property you decide to buy. What happens to your property if something happens to you? Make sure it's what you want to happen, not what your state of residence wants.

Preserving a Family Home

This actually takes on two different yet related perspectives. Many people are in the position in life when an upward or downward move is the next stage.

Perhaps the home you bought when you were single is not going to be sufficient now that you have children. It is amazing—I always thought the starter home we had was more than enough space for children. How much stuff does your kid really need that one room won't hold? If you are chuckling right now, you have the same image in your head that I do. Holy smokes. They say that every child is born with 1,000 square feet of stuff, so for every child you need an extra 1,000 square feet. I know it's not true, but it kind of is.

Here is my point: why not use your first starter home as a rental? Find a way to keep that home either for one of your college fund homes or for a home to help fulfill one of the other needs you may have. I have a client who works for an international company. About every five years or so, the company moves him and his family. He has three rental homes now. When he goes into a new position in a new place, he purchases a home as a primary, lives in it, and then keeps it as a rental when he moves on. He has a management company to handle his properties in each city, and when he transfers, he works with Realtors® to find homes that will be both nice to live in and great investments down the road. As mentioned earlier, choose your Realtor® specific to the experience you need, an expert not just in a location but also in investment. They have to know the area and the opportunities.

Sometimes you are downsizing. The kids are living on their own, and you have extensive equity in the home where you raised them. With the right amount of equity, you have some options. You can tap into those options to fund other things. But specifically, if you have the liquidity, a great option is to rent out the home you are leaving and go ahead and purchase your next one. In many cases, your old home is paid for or close to it. You can keep it as a source of income, and you know the value of its location and feel confident that another family will find it the same from a rental perspective. It's a great way to start getting into the rental business. You know the area and the benefits, but even more confidently, you know the house.

You know the ups, downs, ins, and outs since you had been living there and can have a real good feel for what has or could go wrong or right. You know the reasons why you lived there, and you truly are an expert in the location.

The majority of private investors have their rental homes within a ten-mile radius of where they live. So the best way to describe this style might be love the one you're with. Look at advertising the home to the audience who is moving into your neighborhood. If you look close, you will see yourself in them. More than likely the family makeup and age of children will be similar to when you bought the home. Yes, preferences in design will be different, but there will be many core things about the house and neighborhood that will be the same. To make them comfortable, paint it their colors and empty it out if Grandma's inherited furniture is everywhere. Let the prospective tenant see themselves living there instead of moving into "your house."

You may be in the fortunate position of inheriting a family home. This gift comes from good estate planning, and it's awesome because many times I see these homes come to families without any mortgage or debt. Sometimes multiple siblings have to decide the disposition of the home, and of course, if they can't decide or buy each other out amicably, then they tend to sell. But many times, these homes are in families that don't want to let go, so they turn Mamaw and Papaw's home into a money maker. Yes, some renovations usually need to be done—paint, carpet, and more. And, yes, it will help you get more rent if you remove the dated wallpaper—the one with ducks wearing bonnets and sitting on top of cotton gins. Orange shag is also currently unpopular. I have noticed that many of these estate homes have beautiful hardwoods and features lying underneath the colored shag, and with little money, the kitchens and bathrooms can be transformed. They don't make them like they used to, but wood paneling looks good painted, and a little bit of investment can pay dividends in rental returns.

Most of them are ranches, and that opens them up to a big audience. With baby boomers aging, it's a great target.

Building Wealth and Independence

Real estate investment offers both cash flow and appreciation. If cash flow is less important to you than building wealth (because real estate is not your full-time gig), then it's an especially interesting approach to take, not just for the tax implications as we will discuss later, but also for the appreciation of the asset over time. It's amazing that you can purchase something that, over time, can appreciate at an average rate of 4 to 5 percent just because you woke up and had it in your possession. In some areas, appreciation is even greater, but for argument's sake, be conservative in your projections.

Know that things go up and down. That is why I look at real estate in five- and ten-year increments to evaluate and refine my strategy. Ask yourself: what has the neighborhood or area done in the past five and ten years? And what projections can you make for the next five and ten? If it appreciated in the past five years, what is happening to the area that could make it go up in the next five, or is that growth tapped out? Have you built about as much wealth and appreciation as the real estate asset can take? Is it better to capture your profits and move them to a property with similar potential or with different upward potential due to area changes or types of properties or migration to the area? How do you predict this? You look at trends of an area over one-, three-, and five-year periods and the gains that ensue. You look at potential, which means schools, growth, infrastructure, amenities—you name it. Each positive thing can impact your thought process. But primarily the goal is to have a measure of appreciation built into your total equation. Make some candid mathematical and knowledge-based assumptions about the area. Remember to keep the emotion out of it, and make sure your goal is clear. Cash flow is important, but you are purchasing the property for its ability to appreciate over time, and that is not dependent on paying down your mortgage. Of course, someone else paying down your mortgage is another way to look at wealth building. Someone else making my payments is something to get really excited about, in my opinion. I love that plan.

Building a Safety Net from Your Job

I didn't think I was going to talk about this one. But I could not avoid what I feel is a compelling topic in today's world and society. Most people do not spend a lifetime at the same job, get the gold watch at retirement, and live the high life doing woodworking in the garage making chairs and tables as Christmas presents. Social Security, a retirement vehicle we all pay into, may or may not be around when we need, want, or deserve it. And many companies change their boards, are taken over, bring in their "own people," or stuff just happens, and you find yourself out of a job.

When I was twenty-three years old, I was working as a shipping clerk for a company in Cincinnati, Ohio, where my father was president. I typed invoices and bills of lading for shipping goods internationally. I was going to college at night trying to finish up my degree. I worked out of the headquarters office and was sure that you can't get more secure than working where your own dad is the president. Surely you would never have to worry. Wrong. I remember being called to a meeting on a Friday at noon where we were told the company was shutting down its headquarters and moving to another location. My dad ran the meeting, and he was looking at me knowing I was shocked. He was unable to tell me. I mean, come on, Dad, dang. Anyway, it turned out to be a good thing. Shortly after, I got a job selling 35 mm slides for presentations, and it launched my career in advertising. The clerk job was a dead end, and I knew it. But I did get to watch my dad set an example for his son, which I have carried with me always. Pretty cool. He made the decision that needed to be made, even if it hurt. Sometimes as owners of property, we have to also make those kind of hard decisions. The ability to say "no" sometimes seems to run against our nature, but "no" can be one of the best things we can say in some situations. Sometimes saying no costs money, but in the end, the truth is that the price of yes may be way more expensive in more ways than just money.

Many years later, I remember telling my wife at one point that we had enough rental income coming in that I knew our mortgage on our home would be paid. It is a means to some security as life pronounces its path or if you are embarking on a new path the Lord has in store.

It can also provide you with the ability to change careers. Get your real estate practice started part time and gradually transition to full time. You can't be half-pregnant though—to be successful, you eventually need to commit. That may mean you are not paid for a while, but a transition gives you the ability to build a sustainable career or business. I love this approach.

Tax Planning

It was really hard here not to use the word "avoid." A better way to say it is really "defer." You are going to pay taxes one way or another, so it's really a matter of when, not what.

A few really good tools are available that I want to discuss. I know well and good that I am not here to give tax advice, so call your CPA for the latest and greatest information. I am not a CPA, but I did have a good night's sleep last night.

One great opportunity with property investment is the ability to depreciate the asset on your taxes. Many people utilize this tool with investment property over various terms, and this is a huge part of their planning process. When purchased, each property has a basis. This is a tax term that refers to the base price or value for the property or asset shown on your tax return for the purposes of tax, depreciation, or transfer. This basis is then depreciated annually, and when you sell, that basis is the value used to determine what your gain is and the amount you are taxed on over and above your basis. This is the simple explanation, but truly it's a way to defer your other tax liabilities by a deduction annually on the descending basis or reduce a piece of property as it ages and receive a deduction for it. The textbook definition of "tax basis" for investment property is: *the amount of your capital investment in property for tax purposes. Use your basis to figure depreciation, amortization, depletion, casualty losses, and any gain or loss on the sale, exchange, or other disposition of the property.* In most situations, the basis of an asset is its cost to you. Again, just know when you sell you will pay taxes

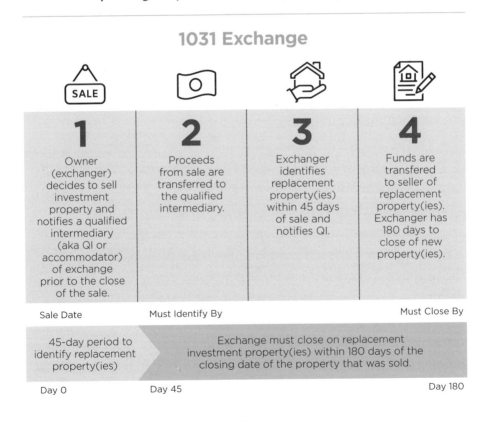

1031 Exchange

1	2	3	4
Owner (exchanger) decides to sell investment property and notifies a qualified intermediary (aka QI or accommodator) of exchange prior to the close of the sale.	Proceeds from sale are transferred to the qualified intermediary.	Exchanger identifies replacement property(ies) within 45 days of sale and notifies QI.	Funds are transfered to seller of replacement property(ies). Exchanger has 180 days to close of new property(ies).

Sale Date	Must Identify By		Must Close By
45-day period to identify replacement property(ies)	Exchange must close on replacement investment property(ies) within 180 days of the closing date of the property that was sold.		
Day 0	Day 45		Day 180

on the difference between the current basis for the property and the amount over that value that you sell for, unless you do a tax-free exchange (commonly known as a 1031 exchange).

I love tax-free exchanges. They give you the ability to take that real estate gain and move it forward into a similar type of real estate and defer the tax. You can spend more than the sale amount for your new property. Basically, you pay the tax eventually when you sell and can also use a loan to move it forward. Below are some parameters for tax-free exchanges:

- You can designate up to three exchange properties for each property you sell.
- You can designate up to 200 percent of the tax-deferred 1031 amount of sale.
- Within forty-five days from date of close, you must identify the properties you will buy.
- Then within six months from date of close, you must purchase the identified property/properties.
- You must do the exchange in a like kind—investment for investment.
- You can designate a part of your funds and pay tax on what is left.
- The timing refers to calendar days, not business days.
- It is imperative you use a qualified intermediary. You never touch the money. If it flows through you, you are not eligible.
- You can do a third-party exchange, which means it is owned by a third party until funds are available.

Last (and obviously), the expense you may have in relation to the property, from interest to property management fees, may be deductible. That makes good sense to me. If I improve or repair a property, depending on the improvements, I will either be able to deduct it from my tax liability, or it will be added to my basis for use against any tax liability. It's a great way to stretch an investment. I know that interest on the loan and insurance and other things that apply may be a great option for you to know more about as you evaluate your spending and returns. Some people really don't understand how much this plays into the returns on an investment. It is a big number in many cases. When you add up these tax benefits, or what I call "soft dollars," it can really help reduce other hard dollar tax liabilities and come back to you in a real form of hard currency.

Saving for Retirement

Well, that's a popular category—cash flow to supplement your steady and stable Social Security or retirement check. You know as well as I do that cash flow for your retirement means freedom to even begin to retire. Freedom goes hand in hand with so many of these reasons to invest, but personally I know that it not only takes a village to raise a child but also takes many different avenues to fund retirement. Social Security is certainly one of them for the optimists, but that check may not be enough, and Social Security may not be around throughout your retirement years. And if all you have is liquidity that is not fluid or productive, you take a pretty large risk in outliving your liquid investments as you never know the life events that make dipping into your pot of money necessary. Some folks take their homes and do reverse mortgages to create cash flow along with other things like annuities, and it creates a great plan.

I don't know that many of us really see ourselves retiring, but we do see ourselves with the ability to slow down, travel, and enjoy life. I know someday soon my time will come to wear shorts with high athletic socks and dress shoes. Not! But I do see a day when I have the flexibility to give more of my time and dictate how I spend the time I have left. This is what retirement planning is really for—enjoying life how we see fit.

I spend time with my financial planner incorporating real estate, and he is very astute and encourages a good blend as a part of my retirement strategy. If you don't have someone like that, look for it. It's a great way to fund your retirement expenses as well. I worked with my planner to figure out, with a degree of annual increase, what my living expenses would look like in the future and made sure I had the appropriate cash flow to match those expenses. I am on my way there, and I know how much I need of what and where it resides (in a trust, an LLC, my personal name, etc.).

A Place to Live in Retirement

I have a client who sold their beach rental house and is doing a tax-free exchange. We looked at all types of investment property from office to townhomes. One strategy that we explored really surprised me. We previewed age-restricted neighborhoods that allowed rentals. This is a really good strategy whether you are doing it for yourself or

Stabilizing Your Retirement with Real Estate

1 Threats to Your Pot O' Money

- Medical care
- Other family in need
- Kids
- Emergencies
- Market fluctuations
- Instability

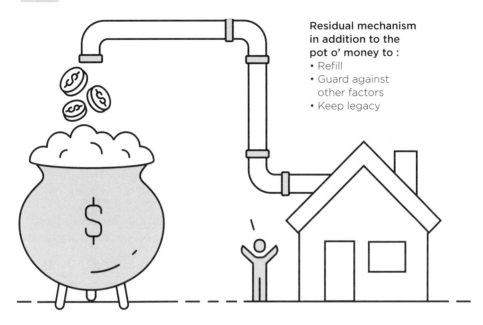

Residual mechanism
in addition to the
pot o' money to :
• Refill
• Guard against
  other factors
• Keep legacy

just as an investment. My client's thinking was that they really were not ready to retire but wanted to identify a place where they would like to live when the time came. That is the key. Thinking on a broader scale, you can purchase a rental in another state, at the beach, or a smaller home that you identify as potentially meeting the needs you anticipate in the next phase of your life. It absolutely will be something to look at if you have some idea what and where you may want to be. Remember if it is a resort property, it does not stop you from visiting or using it with restrictions, but for this purpose we are looking strategically at a place you may want to make your next home. What a great idea.

Paying for Something Else Unrelated

I have an ongoing concern about the cost of health care. I know I am not the only one, and as an entrepreneur, I don't have a cushy corporate health plan or retirement fund. I pay my own premiums, and man-oh-man are they expensive. I am worried about keeping up with long-term care and health-care expenses, so I have a part of my investment cash flow projections specifically built around health-care costs for premiums or ongoing care in the event of something happening.

Others may have a different take on this. Investment cash flow could be earmarked for other forthcoming expenses, from helping your children, funding a trust, buying something else, or for pushing forward to purchase another property. I have heard many different reasons. Sometimes investment property is even a place to keep parents or children who need an extra hand close by. You name it. Just know that real estate can help fund the life you envision. Real estate is one of those things that is truly not as liquid as other assets and can't just be sold in an hour. But it has other qualities that make it possible to access liquidity or borrow against it without a total loss of the asset.

Because You Like it

Let's not forget life is about getting up in the morning and enjoying what we do. If real estate is your passion and you find it an industry that brings you joy, do it. I left a career in advertising that brought me joy for a long time, but I always had an interest in real estate. And as an investor, I did not have to leave my current job to enjoy it. I just had to find good partners to handle the part of the business I did not want to handle. I know parts of it are not always as glamorous or easy, but what career or life choice always is? If you find that career, you let me know.

For some, real estate investing is a hobby, and for others it's a way of life. For me, it's not just my job; it's a real passion. I like to figure out what makes a house unique, where the opportunity is, where to look for value, and how to shape a rental house in a way that makes it rewarding for everyone and meets my clients' personal objectives and mine.

Recently I had the privilege of purchasing someone's family home for an investor. They were adopting some children from Russia. For the record, that made nine kids. Yes, you heard me right—nine kids. They needed to sell the home in order to pay off the loan they had taken to cover the costs of the long, arduous process of adoption. I believe they spent about $35,000. They wanted to enter this next phase of their life debt free. They loved their home, loved their kids' schools, loved their neighbors—they loved everything but, loved being out of debt more. So my investor purchased their home and struck a deal to let them lease the house until their kids finished school. Everyone wins. What can be better than that?

To Give Money Away or Help Others

Many of us are called to give. Sometimes who we give to can change at the blink of an eye, just like the motivation to buy a house can change if a family situation changes. I have dear friends who have a daughter who needed their help caring for her child while she was at work. They watched their grandchild and loved every minute, but the drive to their daughter's house was just too much for them daily. Lo and behold, the house across the street from their daughter came up for sale. I remember it like it was yesterday. My client looked me square in the eye and said, "I want this house, Paul. Do you understand? I want this house." Well, they got that house, and Mimmi (as she is called) lives across the street from her daughter. They have been long-time investors, and now, they made an investment in their daughter and granddaughter and along the way got a pretty nice house as well.

Your passion may mean you want to fund a mission or just feel compelled to give more money away to places and parts of the world that pull your heart strings. They call that "coming from contribution," and it does not matter who is coming into that contribution; it just matters that you have the mindset to do so. Real estate investing can be shelter to a family or someone in need, or even a break for someone to rebuild their credit. I have someone I helped rebuild their life and overcome a hard time in a house. They now are back on their feet and back home thriving. Yes, not everyone appreciates what we contribute, but it is not about that. It's about the fact that we all have needed a hand, and if we haven't yet, the day will come. I guarantee it.

As a Vacation Place

This is an area that my wife and I have learned so much from. In the introduction, you read about my quest in Florida—the good, the bad, the purchase of air. Well, I want to share with you how vacation rentals can really be more intentional. This can be a haven for your family, a way to create a place where you can go and enjoy your time together on a whole new level.

Our properties in Florida were great when we had our own plane and access. Still, we only visited two to three times per year, and the access and touch with these properties was not nearly as easy as others can be. Wanting a beach property if you live in Wisconsin is not going to be an easy commute no matter where you go. But if you find solace or retreat in an area that is reachable in five hours by car, it can make a huge difference in some of the results you may achieve. You also have access to your properties to handle an angry renter, an emergency situation, or a con from someone fabricating an issue. More on that in chapter 15.

As a Career

Make sure you know this is what you want to do. With investment property as a hobby or investment, you can surround yourself with people to help you create and build wealth and a portfolio. But as your career, it's a whole new ballgame. For me, the most important thing when I reached that threshold was to surround myself with smart people, and I affiliated my business with a firm I thought would help with that. It's a wonderful career, but it takes time. If you are just starting out, it takes six months to a year just to get a couple of deals rolling. Be patient; slow and steady wins the race.

The real estate field is ever changing and offers you the opportunity to be fluid, and there are resources available to study trends. Some of the larger cities have local papers that publish extensive real estate data. This book does not focus on flipping houses, but that can be a great career with great risk versus reward potential; you make your most money when you buy. Investment real estate is the same, but you make your money over time. Just like relationships, the buy-and-hold strategy gets better with age. Real estate is a wonderful career, but it's not like selling insurance. Once you sell your family member a home, they may not need one for a while, and they are only going to pay you once. Investment real estate, however, makes money in many ways. The doors to profitability and personal freedom open in many directions with diverse options. It is the gift that keeps on giving for sure.

Important Note: Pick Your Realtor® Carefully

A ton of Realtors® are out there to choose from. Just like there are multiple types of personalities, Realtors® have different skill sets. When buying a home for your permanent residence, certainly local knowledge, value expertise, and alignment with your budget and lifestyle are clear skills required to do a good job. Buying an investment property is a whole different story, and a different set of skills divides the two. That line of expertise and skill takes the shape of your *why*.

Buying your residence is an emotional purchase that fits your individual lifestyle and your needs and wants for functionality and value. Whereas buying an investment requires you to take off the emotional hat, put on your experience hat, and analyze the decision based on a variety of factors. It isn't always good to be a new Realtor's® first customer. This is especially true when it comes to buying investment property. You might argue: how do people get experience if they don't have a first? Let me tell you how: they have mentors. Work either with an experienced Realtor® or one who has an experienced mentor. Here are some interview questions to ask potential Realtors®:

- How do they analyze property?
- What is their thinking and mindset for the market?
- How many investors are they working with currently?
- Do they manage property?
- How many investment properties do they personally own?
- What is their investment philosophy?
- What do they look for?
- What is the process like?
- What do they see happening five to ten years down the road?
- What happens if a property is not listed?
- How do they find properties?

If they know the answers and you like their answers, you got a good one. If they hesitate, ask more questions.

As a Realtor® who works with investors, I turn the tables and interview the investor as well. I don't want to waste my time with someone who sees this as a way to just look at houses for fun. My time is very valuable, and every good agent knows that this is not a business full of pink stars and blue diamonds, where unicorn properties for $50,000 less than asking price are waiting at every corner. It's hard work. If the prospect is searching for unicorns, I will pass.

I always ask clients, "What would make this a success in your eyes?" I also ask them, "How would you like me to communicate with you? How much do you want to be involved? When are you ready to start? How much are you wanting to spend, and how much liquidity do you have? Is the money coming from another source? If so where? Are you willing to meet with a lender now?"

Last but not least is personality. If you don't work together well or communicate or align in expectations, it may be better to pass. I know it's hard to say no—you have a breathing, experienced Realtor® or prospect right in front of you. But sometimes, an honest and quick "no" is a great gift you can give each other.

Special Note for Real Estate Agents Reading This Book

You must know how to guide a client to a place where you understand their goals for investing. Take note: the shows on television make it seem easy to buy and flip. But that is a very risky game for you and them. Remodeling a whole house, adding a room, and/or transforming the kitchen and bathrooms for $10,000 into what even some luxury homes lack is complete foolishness.

Once the client's goals are established, make sure you align yourselves with good vendor partners. If it's tax issues, have a go-to CPA for all of the tax needs. Many times, folks ask whether to put all the properties into a trust or an LLC. Don't be the lawyer. Partner with an attorney who can help your clients get the right advice based on the protection or risk level they seek. Make sure you also align with a good lender or 1031 provider. Just like Realtors®, many lenders are not qualified or don't want to mess with investment property. They just want to sell or refi the family home. Get with a good lender (preferably three to give clients options). Also, just as important is your insurance agent. A strong insurance company partner can provide insight on how to protect the asset from all the pitfalls and surprises the property rental business can dish out over time. If they don't have experience in the rental market, don't be shy about moving on. Note: always read the insurance policy; there are clauses in the policy you need to be aware of that can disqualify coverage.

If you want to get more involved in the investment side of real estate, find a mentor. Find someone you may know or meet someone who will teach you and let you shadow them. If you come across an investor, bring your mentor in to help. Pay them for their time and expertise. I get so upset with agents who don't understand this concept. Get someone on your team who can help you. Remember that if it works and if the transaction successfully meets the investor's goal, they will do more, and of course they will tell others. GET A MENTOR! Don't just read about investing and believe that makes you an expert.

Books, even this one, are simply guides. There is no better education than doing things for yourself when you are working with someone else's money. It's better to give up a little to get that education. It's the newest form of leverage that doesn't require a bank—surrounding yourself with those who can make you better and get you on the experience path faster with fewer failures.

Also, practice what you preach. Buy a rental. It will be an eye-opener for you. Take yourself through the process a few times and learn by doing in the school of hard knocks. It's the best education you can get from "You University."

Know Your Why
Key Takeaways

Know your why before investing in real estate. This is not a get-rich-quick business, but it can offer multiple levels of returns and outlets to defer taxes and create income. But you won't understand the returns unless you understand what you're working toward.

Work with a Realtor® who specializes in investment property to help you select the right property for your goals.

If you are a Realtor®, help your clients be clear on their reasons for investing and help them set expectations for each of those reasons. At every listing appointment ask yourself: should I sell it or buy it, or should they keep it as a rental?

Notes

Success in managing
tenants, owners, people,
and business lies in
the speed and
completeness of
how you communicate.

CHAPTER 2

Communicate Effectively

Communication is an evolving and sometimes nebulous concept. Growing up, my family had a home with a "party line." For those who don't know, a "party line" was when several homes shared a single phone line. You could hear a neighbor pick up and listen—their hand over the receiver couldn't mask the decibels of a barking dog, sneeze, or random outburst. When I finally got up the nerve to call a girl on the phone growing up, I had two sisters who wouldn't hesitate to get on the line and interrupt with, "Get off the phone now. I need to make an urgent call."

In today's world it seems that people have lost the knack for talking, especially younger generations who grew up with cell phones and the thumb activity involved in unlimited texting. I even have a ninety-three-year-old father who texts. Geez, what is this world coming to? Meanwhile, after almost thirty years of marriage, my wife can read my mind and just know what I want or need without a single whisper—no communication needed. (Yeah, right!)

This is why I decided to talk about communication in an investment book. If you run a company, live with children, are married, have a career—you name it—the simple communications cycle I will describe can help make the difference between success and perceived failure (which is the same as real failure once it's perceived). For our purposes, I'll share examples in the property management and investment sense. Once you get the concept, apply it to the situation of your choosing and see if I am correct. It pretty much works anywhere.

First, I want to explain how this concept originated. I am blessed to have a very competent staff. They operate well as a team and are also individually strong in their designated roles. They are truly focused on giving our clients the best customer service they can. One day, we were talking about how I continuously received calls from clients who said they did not know whether their requests for repairs, issues, or challenges were handled per their request as they had not heard anything from anyone. I could easily see in our system when the client had called, how it was handled, and when the task was completed. So I would go back to the client and say, "Well, of course it was handled." Even tenants were posting negative social media comments that we didn't respond to their requests and didn't get back to them on whatever they wanted us to do. Something was missing. So I began to simplify and break down our communication process into a simple cycle, and my staff was stunned by how simple it really is.

The Communication Matrix™

1

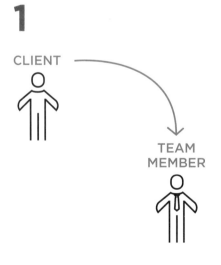

CLIENT

TEAM MEMBER

A tenant or owner or other originator of the request (let's just call them the client) calls or emails with a request—any request. We will assume in this example that the call or email is routed to the correct team member, and the team member understands the request.

2

The team member calls the vendor, schedules the maintenance, makes the appointment, arranges for a quote, looks up a copy of the lease—whatever is required to fulfill the request. It is now on the way to being resolved and has a path do so. The request is not just sitting—it's moving forward.

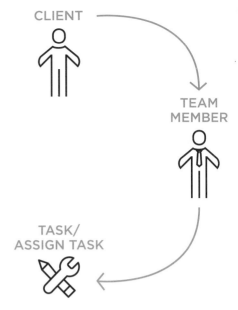

3

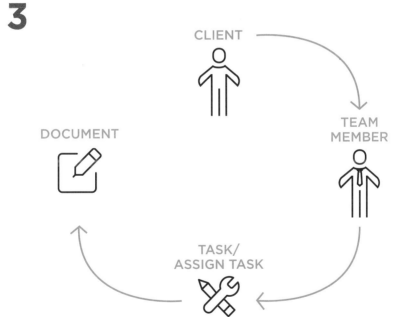

Here's an acronym to learn, live, and love—CYA (cover your a**). In the business of contracts, tenant rights, compliance, and just straight-up memory, it's always best to write it down. We use a cloud-based system that documents all communication we have with vendors, tenants, and owners. It keeps us on top of tasks until they are complete. Documentation can take many forms, including calendar items, sticky notes, electronic journals, or task software—whatever works best for you.

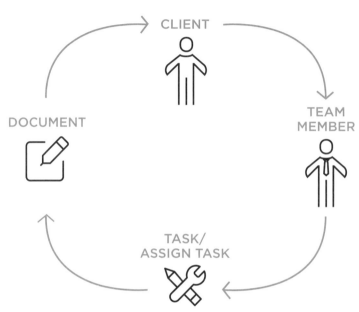

What starts with the client ends with the client. Pretty simple, right? You tell them, "Yes, the task was handled, and this was the outcome." Of course, you could add many layers of documentation to this whole cycle, but the beauty is its simplicity. It starts with the client and ends with the client. *DONE and DONE!*

If you don't follow the full cycle, however, simple can become complicated quickly. After careful thought, we realized we were not completing step 4. Our inherent nature to just handle it (steps 1 through 3) was happening with a very high level of success, but step 4 was regularly not happening. *Failure comes if the client calls you to ask what is happening before you call them. At that point, you have lost credibility even though the request has been fulfilled.*

In almost every case, we were completing the task, or the task was in the process, and we had nothing to report. So here are a few simple rules to the Communication Matrix™:

1. Communication begins and ends with the client.
2. You can circle around the matrix multiple times, but you cannot stop until you reach the client for the final time with a final result.
3. No news to report is still news to talk about.
4. Multiple cycles can happen over the same task, but the same rules apply. For example, one cycle could be in process with a tenant while a similar process is underway with the owner.
5. Copying the client on documentation puts you in your strongest position.

The place where most people drown is two feet from the edge of the pool. Similarly, the place where most communication fails is one step from the end of the cycle. I believe that success in managing tenants, owners, people, and business lies in the speed and completeness of how you communicate. Many times I have heard business owners of my generation say that if they could get young staff to just pick up the phone and talk to someone, they would be three times more successful. It is a lesson we all need to remember since the other lines of communication are so easy. I am not a hater of texts and emails, but I believe that some things like inflection or intent are not effectively communicated in the written word. I bet you could name many times where someone interpreted something you said in a text or email that was not the way you intended. So here is my soap-box list of preferred communication methods within the matrix.

When the request comes in, give the requester a basis for how you will complete the cycle the first time. For example, "I will call you in forty-eight hours with an update," or "I will check in with you once I have the vendor's schedule, so it may take two days before you hear back from me."

When responding to a tenant, realize that everything is urgent to them. Do not feed their anxiety. If a toilet is clogged, instead of letting them think it's a 911 emergency, you might say one or more of the following: "How do you believe the clog happened?" "Is there another bathroom in the house?" "When is a good time for the plumber to come during the day? Can he enter unescorted?" "In the event it is your fault, how are you going to pay for the plumber visit?" "Please refer to the move-in handbook. This is a nonemergency." "I will call you after the plumber returns my call with his schedule. It can take up to X days for him to respond to non-emergencies. The easier you make your schedule, the faster we can get them there." To complete the loop, notify the client and the tenant of the schedule and then to do the work. The big finish is to tell them both the results.

One of my favorite stories along this line was a tenant with a clogged toilet. To her, it was a major emergency. She insisted that it was the owner's fault and claimed water was pouring out of the toilet and was leaking down the floor. We walked her through how to shut off the water and then called the owner, assigned the task to a plumber, documented the task at hand, set the appointment with tenant, and let the owner know about the plan.

The plumber called me later laughing so hard he could barely talk. While examining the trap in the toilet, he pulled out a Dora the Explorer doll—it was stuck causing a huge backup. The tenant, standing by with her hands on her hips, let the plumber know in no uncertain terms that the doll was not hers and that the previous tenant or the owner must have put it there ... blah ... blah ... blah. About two minutes later, her five-year-old came running into the room, grabbed the Dora doll (ewwww, nasty), and blurted out, "Dora, I am so glad you're back from your pee-pee potty adventure. I missed you."

The cycle ended with the tenant paying for the plumber, the owner and me laughing over the results, and of course the icing on the cake, a welcome-home party for Dora. Children are the greatest example of unfiltered communication on the planet. In some ways I wish we could all keep that kind of unfiltered honesty.

For the real estate agents or property managers who are reading this book, let me add some other fundamental learnings when it comes to this communication cycle. The real estate business like many, has evolved to a place where technology is a necessary tool in order to be successful. It is, however, just a tool—one of many needed to complete the task at hand. *It should not be used when delivering certain messages.* Follow these rules of engagement according to the type of message you need to deliver:

- Never deliver bad news by text or email.
- If you're angry, don't write about it until you call first. (This is sometimes hard to do, but take a deep breath and do it. You won't regret it.)
- If you are concerned how something may be perceived or misinterpreted in an email, you're probably right.
- Texting is best used for yes or no questions about scheduling.
- Even a voicemail is better than nothing. There is actually software out there that allows you to make a call and it will go straight to someone's voicemail. Not what I prefer but at least you can express inflection.
- Don't call someone if they are abusive. This is when text or email is best—like to tell them goodbye forever.
- Document things electronically. Don't be afraid to share it.
- If you call people back quickly, even just to say you can't talk right now but will call in a few hours, you will have more business than you can handle.
- The best form of written communication to close the final loop is a handwritten note. Just be sure to make a copy for your files.
- Pick up the dang phone. If you don't have a local area code, buy a local phone number and forward it to your out-of-state number. You can't appear to be a local expert if your phone number is screaming, "I'm not from around here!"

Communicate Effectively
Key Takeaways

When someone makes a request, communication begins and ends with that person. Simply fulfilling the request, no matter how expertly done, is insufficient without follow through.

"Easy" forms of communication like email and text are not necessarily the best forms of communication. Use the right medium for your message.

Document everything.

Notes

_____

_____

_____

_____

_____

_____

_____

_____

_____

_____

_____

_____

_____

_____

_____

_____

Remember this
above all else:
**you're not living there.
It is an investment.**

CHAPTER 3

Identify Your Investment Property

Buying an investment property requires a different mindset than buying your permanent home. Remember this above all else: *you're not living there.* It is an investment. Certainly you want it to be appealing—you don't want to purchase something that makes you cringe. But you also want to purchase something appropriate for potential tenants, for the demographic attracted to that area. For example, if the home is in an area where the primary density is families because of schools or walkability or amenities or the surroundings, you want that home to appeal to a family.

Another example: I love ranch houses. I think ranch houses are the secret to everything. However, in a lot of families, and especially young families, the parents want to be close to the kids, so they want a two-level home with all the bedrooms close together upstairs. (They'll realize later on that you want your kids' bedrooms as far away as possible.) They typically don't want the adorable ranch house I want to retire in, but that day will come, and I'll capture them soon enough.

When you're viewing properties, think about your audience for that neighborhood. It's all about the tenant you're trying to attract.

In part, this goes back to knowing not just your why but also your who. Certain neighborhoods and types of homes are better suited to certain goals. What price point are they in? What kind of setup works well in the neighborhood and has demand? What kind of accessibility do they need to public transportation? Do they need a good school district? How easy is it to get in and out of the neighborhood? What amenities does that ideal tenant need to have nearby to be happy? Some people want to live in a high-rise condo where they put their garbage bag out into the hallway, and the magic garbage fairies pick it up every Tuesday and Thursday. But others want a yard where a dog can run and play.

Don't worry about whether the light fixtures or the flooring appeal to you. Don't focus on the ships-and-kittens wallpaper someone put up in the 1960s. All of those things are cosmetic and can be updated to appeal to your ideal tenant.

Look Ahead

The second thing to remember: *numbers matter, but they're not the only matter.* Even when numbers look good, they may not be good. Let's say you're looking at property that will rent at $800 a month, and purchase costs and expenses will be $100,000. When you multiply rent times twelve and divide by the purchase costs and expenses, you go, "Wow, this looks like a slam dunk investment." And it very well may be, but you also have to consider what happens when that tenant moves out. Historically, in my market in the Carolinas, the most stable rental market is in properties with rents over $1,100 a month. Typically, properties with rents below $1,000 don't turn over in a cheap way when tenants leave. If you evaluate repainting, reflooring, and repairs when each tenant moves out, all of a sudden that investment looks awful inside and out.

Of course, you will evaluate rental rates, the mortgage, your profit, your reserves that you would set aside, tax benefits, and so on. But there are important financial aspects that don't fit neatly in your mathematical equations. How is the neighborhood doing? Is it growing? Have the prices gone up over time? Is the surrounding area undergoing revitalization? What's going on with transportation? What do the jobs look like? Are new industries moving to the area? What restaurants and other amenities are close by? What's the sewer capacity?

Yes, I said sewer capacity. I'm involved in a project right now where they're adding a twenty-four-inch sewer line to an area with an existing eight-inch sewer line. So they'll have thirty-two inches of sewer capacity. That is not just a lot of poop; it's also a sign the community is setting up for the ability to grow.

To make the case, you have to factor in much more than the rent times twelve divided by your purchase cost/expenses. Let's just pretend for a minute that we're going to look at a house. The potential rent on this particular house multiplied by twelve and divided by the amount of money you'll spend on it leaves you with a return of only 6 percent. That doesn't seem like a lot. But then I tell you about the new roads coming in and the big company relocating down the road or the light-rail line planned a few blocks over. Now you see potential that future rent will be higher, and the property will appreciate in value faster.

As stated earlier, I always evaluate properties in a five- to ten-year window. You typically have an up and a down cycle within ten years. That will give you a good idea of how the property will perform. Depending on your goals, your *why*, if nothing has happened during that time, then maybe you need to look somewhere else for a good investment. But if you just want a good, stable property, nothing happening could be a good thing as well. The strategy is always individual, each one is right if it's right for you.

Excel can help you evaluate the numbers to decide whether a property is a candidate for your investment. It can also help you plan your visits to interesting properties. See the sample spreadsheets in the appendix at the end of the book. You can find downloadable versions on my website at pauljamison.com/downloads. Use the password **OiKpJDoNe** to access them.

Do Your Due Diligence

The term "due diligence" can be confusing because it has both a legal meaning in the real estate world and a slightly different meaning in the world at large. *You must do all the discovery you can.* The more common meaning is synonymous with "research" and oh boy a lot of it. In the real estate world, you might think of due diligence as synonymous with "layaway." You're putting the property aside while you do your research.

Research

Don't take any shortcuts in your research. That includes researching property tax rates, HOA rules, area improvements that could affect future property values, and schools if they're important to you. (Note that fair housing rules prevent your Realtor® from commenting or sharing opinions on schools.) Always, of course, call and get insurance estimates that include flood, wind, and hail. As a landlord, consider a good personal liability umbrella to protect you over and above all the other insurance policies. Ask about a CLU report from your insurance agent. A CLU report is like a credit report on a house. It will give you a history of any claims or issues that you may want to know about that could affect your rate. If the home has a history of issues, it's better to know what and when they occurred.

Research doesn't stop there. Your Realtor® should be helping you with these things, but you still need to be aware of all the details and costs that may impact your investment.

As a more unconventional form of research, I like to do drive-bys at different times of the day and week. Standing in front of the home, I look five houses down on the right, five down on the left, and the same across the street. How do they take care of their property? What are they doing to the property? Are cars parked in the front yard? On Saturday night, is there a place to park, or are neighbors parking all over the place? It may not look the same on a Sunday morning when everyone's at church, so go at odd times and look at it.

One time, I was researching a piece of property in downtown Charlotte. I used Google Street View to check out the neighborhood. I placed the little man icon on the map in front of the house and spun him around. It just so happened that when the Google car drove by, a police car was parked in front of the house, and two policemen were standing in the driveway across the street. It looked like they were arresting a man in his driveway. Technology today can certainly be fun when evaluating property.

Use Google Satellite View too to look at the house from above. Check out power lines, creeks, obstructions, and whether the house backs up to a high school. If your tenants aren't ready for Friday night football games and the marching band, they will not enjoy that house.

Buyer beware: nothing is worse than a sneaky photo a real estate agent has taken at an angle that doesn't show the warts. I'd rather see the warts and know them up front because the minute they hide one thing, you have to wonder what else they are hiding. You don't want to drive up and discover a giant metal play set with electric wires hanging off of it, especially if you can hang your plug out the window and turn all your lights on. That's going to be a problem. Use the tools that are available to save yourself time from buying somebody else's problem. Do the inspections; do the due diligence; do the research; and do it at odd and various hours too.

Layaway

In the legal, real estate sense, due diligence is like layaway because you're putting money down to reserve something you think you want, but then you have time to change your mind. Let's say, for example, Kohl's is having a 20-percent-off sale on Crocs. You love Crocs, you love purple, and they have one purple pair left in your size. Now those normally go for $150, but you can get them for $125. Sweet! But you heard Macy's is having a sale too. So you take those $125 pair of Crocs to the layaway window and give them $20, so they'll hold those Crocs for you for two weeks. Well, then you jump in the car and drive over to Macy's. Macy's is having a 60-percent-off sale! Those same Crocs—same size, same color —are only $90. Your choice is clear. So what happens to the pair at Kohl's? They keep your $20 and put those Crocs back on the shelf to sell them to somebody else. Even with the loss of your $20 you still saved money.

Due diligence is a period of time where the buyer has a chance to examine the property and can walk away for any reason—wake up, break a nail, change your mind, and walk away. But just like the Kohl's example, in the case of real estate, that money goes to the seller, and they put the property back up for sale.

In my home market, North Carolina, and many others, when you make an offer on a home, you're essentially putting the home on layaway; this is called the due diligence period. During this time, you perform your home, termite, radon, and other inspections needed; negotiate repairs; get an appraisal; and research the title to make sure the sellers can actually sell the house to you. In return for the due diligence fee, the seller has agreed to take that home off the market so that you can perform any necessary inspections thoroughly. To further clarify, it's more than just plain research because now you have access to the property to evaluate whether it's a good purchase or just best to walk away.

Inspections will happen throughout the life of the property, starting from when you first step inside during a showing prior to even writing a contract for purchase. When I walk into a house, I look at corners to see if the wall is cracking in the areas around the doors and windows. Take special note as well of the direction of the cracking. Are the cracks in a stair step, horizontal, or vertical direction? I look at the floors. Are the boards uneven, or do they have ridges on the side or large gaps? Is there any cupping? If so, there may be a moisture problem of some sort under the house. I look at how the house was maintained. I look under the sinks. I move rugs to look for giant pee stains hidden underneath or a plant that has been over watered and ruined the hardwood floors. I flush the toilets, run the sink, hit the AC—common things you'd do in a home. A lot of times if the AC is super cold, they're covering up a bad smell. Here is where you get your first impression of how much work it will take to get it rent-ready, and then you factor that into your equations.

Once under contract, your official due diligence inspection should be done by a professional third party. A good inspector is thorough but not an alarmist. Today's inspection reports—I'm sad to say—are typically upwards of thirty-nine pages of CYA for the inspector before the inspection even starts.

Don't shortcut the inspection but do understand what's important and what's not. Here's the key: just because it doesn't meet today's code does not mean it's necessarily bad. Building code changes daily. So be aware that a home inspector is giving you an account of today's code. If the circuit breakers are not the same ones that they use today, or if the clearance is not the same, or the stairs don't meet the current code, contact a specialist in that issue to do a safety inspection. You'll need to have a specialist in every category of your world, trustworthy people who won't take you to the cleaners. Your Realtor® should help with introductions.

It's also important that any updates to the home have permits. Have they added a room or a bathroom? Have they finished a basement? If they don't have permits, your insurance company has a reason to deny claims. So ask, look up, and cover your bases.

Negotiating the Price

I think inherently when people wake up in the morning, everybody wants a deal. I can't think of anybody who doesn't. In this particular case, I say you certainly want to pay as little as you can because you make your money when you buy, meaning where you start ultimately affects where you end. If the seller isn't willing to negotiate on price, but the numbers still work, get out of your own way. If it checks all the boxes, the rents look good, the return looks good, and the future looks good, pay what you need to pay. Sometimes I've even paid over asking price in a competitive situation. I had my eye on the future where appreciation would outpace today's higher price.

When you're negotiating, try to look at the situation from all sides and be reasonable. I've been on the seller side and had potential buyers say, "There's a mark on the wall. I want you to repaint the whole wall," or "I don't like the color of the wall. You need to paint it." Go in with this mindset: what if you were on the other side of that transaction? How would you feel, or how would you react? There's something called negotiation fatigue where if you pick too long and if you're petty too long, you wear out the seller, and you lose—you lose big. Do you want price, or do you want terms? Because in the normal world, you can't always have both. Don't negotiate your way right out of a fabulous deal.

The most important thing is never to get in so far financially that you're up against the wall. You should have at least six months of reserves for whatever property you buy. If the idea that it won't rent in thirty days puts you in a state of panic, it is not the right time for you. Wait until you have those reserves. As for what price range to target, look for areas where the rents are in excess of $1,100 a month and where the property will return at least 8 percent gross, meaning before taxes, fees, and insurance. Multiply the rent times twelve and then divide by what the house costs and your initial cash outlay for expenses. If the result is 0.08 or higher, you're in the right ballpark.

Financing

There are multiple ways to finance your investment property. Note that investor rates are usually about a point higher than a normal home purchase rates, depending on your credit. Plan to put down at least 25 percent. Some people use a home equity line on their existing home, and current tax laws provide some benefit for that. Of course, that can change at any given time. Others go to a bank for a mortgage. I always recommend a thirty-year, fixed-rate mortgage. If you want to accelerate your payments, do it on your timing. So if you need some additional cash for a new air conditioner or a new roof, you're not stuck with the higher fifteen-year payment.

Property Outside Your Home Market

The majority of people who invest are buying within a ten-mile radius of their homes, for good reason. When I have had issues at my properties on the coast, it's a four-and-a-half-hour drive to get there and deal with it, and that's a hard day. Property near home is just easier to get to. It's also easier to handle marketing yourself because you know the advantages of your area better than any other market.

That said, there are opportunities outside of your market. I go into vacation rentals in chapter 15, so I'll not go too deeply into that topic here. But I will emphasize that having a good team local to your property is essential. Finding that team needs to be solved before you even start looking at property. Nothing is worse than finding a great deal and watching it go down the tubes without the proper local team behind you.

Two other things to be aware of are taxes and insurance. These issues can give you some nasty surprises if you haven't done your due diligence. Property taxes are different everywhere you go. For example, if you're not a permanent resident of the state where your property is located, you may pay an excessively high amount of property tax, much more than the permanent residents pay. In coastal areas in particular, insurance is a big deal. When you get insurance on the coast, understand what you're signing. When we bought our oceanfront home and then bought insurance, we did not pay enough attention to the fine print that said if a storm with a name damages your property, it changes your deductible to 3 percent of the total property value. So when a tropical depression rolled through, my deductible went from $1,250 to $18,000 thousand just because the storm had a name. Every policy is different, but my point is to read your own insurance policy carefully, and realize that the way the insurance company has written it is usually not in your favor and is loaded with exceptions.

It's OK to Walk Away

Walking away is sometimes a part of doing business. And remember that investing in property is a business. This gets to an emotional piece of this business that is hard for some people. Be prepared to spend $1,000 to $1,500 on due diligence. It's worth it because you might lose way more than that if it's a bad investment. Go in with a mindset that if you hit a snag you can't work through, walk away. It's OK. It has to be OK. It's the cost of doing business.

Identify Your Investment Property
Key Takeaways

Selecting an investment property isn't about your wants and needs. It's about your future tenant's wants and needs.

Numbers matter, but they're not the only matter.

Be thorough in your due diligence. Due diligence is a period of time where the buyer has a chance to examine the property and can walk away for any reason. It's OK to walk away.

Notes

Spend to the trend

in the neighborhood
and area.

CHAPTER 4

Get the Property Rent-Ready

Congratulations! You now hold the keys to the first of hopefully many rental properties to come. You have walked through the inspections and financing and done all the evaluation possible to get to this point. Now, let's take some clear steps to getting this home ready to produce results for you.

I remember when I bought my first local rental property. I did not have any resources lined up to update the kitchen, sand the floors, paint, or complete repairs. Someone approached me about staying there for free, and in return, they would do all the repairs needed within ninety days and then would move out. It was someone I knew who needed some help, and I certainly didn't know any better, so I agreed. For the first thirty days, I saw things happening—piles of removed items in the driveway and materials he requested I purchase. I was thinking how much of a genius I was and how much money I would save. Fast forward six months: I was a dope. I realized why most people, especially those of us with kind hearts, fail managing their own properties—because we want to help people and trust they will do everything they say they will do, when they say they will do it. As time went on, I heard much worse stories of disregarded kindness and learned that people don't always care about you as much as you care about them. In my case, the work did get done, just much later than agreed, and I was able to rent the property a week after they left for a great return.

I will take this time though to warn you: do not allow tenants to make improvements to your property. Over all my years, I have seen few situations where that really works. Actually, it makes things worse. Yes, even if they are family members and you're feeling the ultimate pull on your heart strings, it is not a good idea to enter into a repair or upgrade commitment for reduced or deferred rent. If you are forced to do it, however, don't give them the deferral until the work is done. Don't make the mistake of giving them money for materials either. The best practice is to buy the materials yourself or reimburse with an approved receipt. Any leftover materials should be returned, and you should be refunded. At least you control the risk a bit more and ensure where your money goes.

Now that we've established you don't let a tenant or family member help you get the home rent-ready, here's how you do get a house ready to rent.

Rent-Ready Rules

1. Change all the locks on the exterior doors to a quick-set system. Change the keys the moment you get control of the property. Do not pass go; do not collect $200—change all exterior locks right away.
2. Meet the neighbors. Let them know you are the new owners and your plans for property improvements. They may not be happy they are living next to renters, but if you're managing it yourself, give them your info and make them feel comfortable that you actually care about the home and who goes in it.
3. Complete upgrades and repairs. If you are managing the repairs yourself, get your team of handy folks together

and have them ready to swarm in. You should have given them a walk-through or at least a heads-up before you closed, so you could coordinate what you needed right after closing. If you are using a management company, get them over to walk the property and review what needs to be done to get it ready and to discuss timing and marketing. They have experience, so they may be able to save you from spending money in the wrong areas.

4. Make the yard great. It's an easy first step to making you money, and landscapers are often the easiest resources to get to work right away. This is especially important if, after you said, "I do," the seller decided to stop maintaining the yard. As a practice, I take pictures of the before and after, which helps me remember improvements made and keeps me aligned with what I have done.

5. Go to the bank and open a separate account for this property. This way you can keep track of rents, expenses, and returns. If you are self-managing, make sure you open a separate account for the tenant's security deposit as you are not allowed to intermingle your funds with theirs.

6. Clean only after all your other work is done. I always recommend turning over a home with a deep clean, including freshly cleaned carpets. Hang on to receipts and take pictures of how the home looked before tenants moved in. They should return it the same way (with normal wear and tear of course).

7. Don't show the property till it's ready. Most of the time, even though you tell prospective tenants what is left to do, they complain about what is left to do. Wait. It will pay off, and they will appreciate the home and the process more.

8. Purchase a landlord's insurance policy and a general liability umbrella to protect you from a wide variety of damages and, as the word "umbrella" implies, to broadly protect you from the raining risks of tenant injury or claims.

Upgrades and Repairs

In almost every house we buy, we see common threads of what needs to be repaired or upgraded. Once the house is empty, you see all of the blemishes and imperfections previous owners craftily covered with furnishings and other artwork or distractions. When I look at houses, I pull up rugs and look around plants and garbage cans. In one house, they had an oddly placed blanket in the bathtub—yes, you are reading this right, a blanket—to make it look like a "spa bath." Nope. A huge hole had been punched in the tub and covered in resin and an absolutely absurd repair job. The most common damage previous owners hide is when they overwater plants on the hardwood floors or dog accidents seep under the rug. Doors and walls with holes are also easy to miss until the house is completely empty. And let's face it—movers and friends-turned-movers are not the kindest to the walls on the way out.

Following are some of the most common upgrades to get you the most money on your rent. Note that this can vary from house to house and area to area.

Paint

A fresh coat of paint goes a long way to making a home rent-ready. When people move out, you see the blemishes, holes from pictures, scuff marks, and hand and dirt prints. Here is the simple argument for fresh paint: you can be certain no marks were on the wall before your tenants moved in. You win by default. Fresh trim also makes a home pop.

Use light colors and scrap the accent-wall idea. Every room should be the same, every room equal in the eyes of paint. But stay away from yellow—only 26 percent of the population likes yellow, so make a better pick. Some homes have children's rooms with children's themes. I know what you're thinking—someone may like it. Odds are not in your favor. Teenage girls do not like My

Little Pony even if they like horses. Then they paint over it with black or orange, and you deal with a mess. Paint it. Move on.

Floors

If the floor and carpet are in good shape, clean them and remove all stains. If a pet odor surfaces when you clean, remove and replace the pad if the cost makes sense. For the record, in the best cases, carpet only lasts three years, so be prepared to replace it in three years no matter what. If you get longer from it, great, but don't count on it. Take all the carpet out of wet areas such as bathrooms, the kitchen, and the laundry room. If you want to save money, put carpet in bedrooms and upper levels, but leave high-traffic areas with hard flooring.

I also look at real hardwood floors as a blessing and a curse. If you allow pets, hardwood floors are easy to clean and keep allergens low but get scratched really easily. I put luxury vinyl plank (LVP) on top of hardwoods if I have the budget. It lasts forever, is virtually bulletproof, and looks wonderful. You have tons of styles to choose from and can give your home a real luxury look. Then when you're ready to sell, remove the floating LVP and sand and polish the hardwoods for a really great look. I just covered a set of hardwood floors in a house where the floors had been covered by green and orange shag since the house was built in 1970. The hardwoods underneath had never been walked on. Now the LVP will take me through the growth and renting years with no worry.

Plumbing

This is a no-compromise area. Any leaks or other water issues inside and out must be solved and stopped. Water is a biggie—don't cut corners here at all. If you are on a well, have the water heater drained and cleaned by a professional. If you didn't test the water at purchase, do it now. You can treat a tainted well, but knowing it's tainted is half the battle.

Lights

Yes, sometimes lights need changing. I suggest LED fixtures to minimize the maintenance and maximize the lighting. For the best prices, I go to Habitat ReStore, or I buy lighting sets from the big box stores, so all the fixtures look alike. Change all the bulbs and make sure all the lights work. Again, when they move in, they can't argue if your checklist has this done.

Landscape

Make sure the yard is clean and ready. Again, you give it to them how you want it back. Standard leases require the tenant to handle leaves, mowing, blowing, and yard trimming. This does not include bush trimming in some cases. If you want to make sure the yard gets maintained and you have no issues or HOA violations, get it handled by a landscape company and add it to the rent. Don't do it yourself—they will just corner you and complain.

Remotes and Smoke Detectors

All should be present and accounted for: two remotes for the garage, and carbon monoxide (CO) and smoke detectors in appropriate areas.

HVAC

Get the HVAC serviced two times per year and change all the air filters monthly. Services are available that will send filters to your rental property monthly, right to the door. Purchasing a home warranty is a good idea because right when you start, you can show the HVAC was serviced and was operating. No preexisting conditions. It gets things started right. We do a service on all our units in spring and fall. Filters are checked at inspection. Recently, thanks to a good home warranty, a troubled system was fully replaced for $1,600. That's a deal!

Tenant Checklist and Instructions

Note any dings or scratches before the tenant moves in. We provide tenants a checklist (as you will see later) that they return to us. Take pictures of everything and keep them for your records. Nothing beats a picture. Also give your renter a set of instructions for care, such as products that can and can't be used on hardwood floors or how to clean the ovens or carpets. You can post the care list inside a kitchen cabinet.

Spend to the Trend

This is where some help from a property manager is critical. The first thing to remember is that you are not living there. You spend to the trend. What that means is you spend based on rental amount and trends in the neighborhood and area. You don't put granite countertops in every rental. You don't put vinyl in every rental either. You look at the commonality of neighborhood, understand what is expected, and you upgrade to that level. You don't do it based on your personal taste. It can be hard to do, but it's an investment, and you don't want to underspend either. If your budget does not allow for a particular upgrade, plan for it in the future and tell the tenant that in six months you will, for example, replace the dishwasher. I find that if you hire a property manager, they can help you prioritize spending in the areas that matter to tenants to make the home shine.

Initial Documentation

Once all your repairs and upgrades are complete, document the condition of the home with a thorough inspection and photos. This initial documentation is the benchmark, the beginning, the way to document your property and how it changes with tenants and time. Make clear notes in a defensible, dated file. Include notes on any preexisting issues you are aware of. Then take pictures—lots of them. Page 144 has a comprehensive step-by-step inspection instructions. Save your notes and the pictures on a thumb drive, date it, and save it in your property file. We also use software to upload these pictures and notes to the cloud to have this benchmark easily available from a mobile device during subsequent inspections.

Staging

Yes, staging rentals is important. Buy some artificial plants (greenery) for the living room or great room, entry way, and dining room, and possibly some small artificial plants in containers for the bath or mantle areas. Also buy a set of new towels and rolls of toilet paper for every bathroom. Towels don't need to be expensive, but use them to accent the colors in the bath, warm it up, make potential tenants feel comfortable. Place a cookbook stand and some decorative oil bottles strategically in the kitchen. Use decorative items around the master bedroom, master bathroom, kitchen, and living room to give the home some life. Just those few simple touches make a huge difference in time to rent. In one of my rentals, I staged the house and rented it immediately, and the renter wanted to buy all the stuff. The real secret to this approach is that you can use these items over and over. Just like when selling a home, staging can make an empty house more inviting. We're not talking about much more than a couple of hundred spent on this. Light staging consists of "sprucing" up the kitchen, bath, and mantle and keeping the windows clean, so you can open the blinds and let the light in. Of course, a deep clean is also a form of staging. Nothing beats a clean house in appearance and smell.

Marketing the Property

WARNING: if you read nothing else, read this! **DO NOT USE CRAIGSLIST!** This is a recipe for disaster. Facebook and Craigslist are the two most heavily hacked sites for rentals. If you have a property manager, the MLS (Multiple Listing Service for Realtors®) is a great way to start getting your property out there. Most property management companies also have sites that integrate with other websites where people search. Here are some other important marketing tips:

- Take at least sixteen pictures, ideally of the staged home, to display with listings. For rentals over $2,000 per month, hire a professional photographer because pictures are your most typical first impression. Statistics show that a decision is made online from the photos 95 percent of the time.
- Put a sign in the yard.
- Distribute a flyer to surrounding employers. By "distribute," I mean go in and talk to someone and then hand them the flyer.
- Hold an open house.
- Only do showings in bulk, meaning schedule multiple people to come at the same time. It creates urgency and works to get it rented quicker with more options. For us, the first application submitted gets first consideration.
- Use directional signs from the main road.
- Always have someone at the showing. Never have someone go unescorted by giving them the code unless they are a licensed agent. Some management companies will give prospective tenants a code in exchange for a copy of their license. Bad idea: the appliances tend to leave when you show like that. You also get great feedback and can overcome obstacles when showing your property in person.
- If you want to protect your property while it's empty, the SimpliSafe alarm is a great way to do that. Con: you'll need Internet turned on to run it. Pros that outweigh the con by far: you can reuse it in different properties and even set it to monitor for leaks behind toilets and refrigerators.
- Talk to your religious institution if you belong to one. They're a great resource.

- Visit the local chamber of commerce or town hall if it's nearby. Talk to someone; don't just leave flyers.
- Call local employment and insurance agencies. I have done well with displaced families whose homes were being rebuilt, and they pay a premium.
- Tell your kids, no, they can't live there.
- If you have an executive-style rental and want to get the largest dollars, advertise to luxury builders. Many people moving into the area or others building luxury homes want a short-term rental while their homes are being built or until they get a chance to look around to decide where they want to live. People often ask me if they should be furnished or unfurnished, and I tell them if it's a condo or townhome and/or you're doing monthly rentals to executives, furnish it. If you are renting to families or couples, the company is usually paying for them to bring their stuff, so keep it empty for your biggest opportunity.

Get the Property Rent-Ready
Key Takeaways

Don't offer free rent in exchange for help getting your property rent-ready, not even to family members down on their luck.

Get the property rent-ready before showing it to potential tenants. They don't need to know about your to-do list. They just need to see a move-in ready home.

Budget for upgrades and repairs based on trends in the neighborhood. Not every home needs granite countertops.

Notes

Don't over-improve
or under-improve
your property.
**Adjust your rent
accordingly.**

CHAPTER 5

Establish the Rent

When I worked for the private real estate fund mentioned in the introduction, the amount of properties we acquired in the Carolinas depended on me evaluating every property and putting forth conservative rent numbers that were used to evaluate the asset. Time was always of the essence. Spreadsheets full of properties to evaluate typically came in about 8 p.m. at night, and I had to have them complete by the next morning. Yes, it really did stink to lose a whole evening with family because I was looking up rental numbers through a variety of tools and then evaluating the averages and similar homes. It was about as much fun as watching paint dry. It felt like a bonus when I had to evaluate two homes in the same neighborhood that had same characteristics.

I also had to stand behind those numbers. If the rental numbers were off, then it put the whole team and assets to investors off. However, some simple leading indicators can drive forward the way you evaluate property and rent to make sure the home has positive cash flow.

Research Comps

Your rental rate is not based on your payment or expenses. I can't tell you the number of times I have been told the rent needs to be

$X because my payment is $Y. If you set your rent this way, you will probably end up losing one way or another. Your payment is not what drives the rental market; demand and the economy do. That means schools, amenities, growth, jobs, the housing market, and so forth. Research comparable properties (comps) with the following tools.

Signs

If there is a home in the same neighborhood, call the number on the sign. Ask them basic information about the house, so you can compare it, and ask them how long it's been vacant.

Neighbors

Neighbors usually know if rental properties are available in the area. You can ask them which houses and if they know anything. This is not always a reliable source and my least favorite.

Realtors®

If you are using one or are related to one (don't let them live there either), they can easily check out MLS for other rentals in your neighborhood. Make sure you match up the bedroom and bathroom count with your property. Square footage should be plus or minus 10 percent for the most accurate comps. When comparing rents, you also have to be careful of older comparisons. The owner may not have raised the rent in years since they felt they had a great renter and didn't want to shift with the upward trend of the market.

Online Tools

Even though online tools like property value websites and public tax records can be unreliable, sometimes they do have data points that can be used for evaluation. Just remember though, they use an algorithm that is not always a good basis, but at least they can give you a +/- $200 range per month.

Rental Sites

Sites like Rentals.com, Zillow.com, Trulia.com, and local property management companies' websites can give you the closest to real data for what things could rent for. If you go to a place like Craigslist, however, you may find yourself comparing your rental to a scammer's page and not a real page that reflects true rental rates.

Judge the Parameters

Here is where your money is really made. Once you get a basis for approximately what that rental amount should be, you need to take a look deeper inside that number.

Location, Location, Location

Look at satellite pictures of the area or drive by the home in the neighborhood you're comparing yours to. Make sure you're not comparing your property to one with a big electric tower in the back yard or one that is the first home in the neighborhood. Make sure you understand where it's located and that you are doing the best you can to compare that price and how it affects rent. Cul-de-sac homes pull a much higher number, just like they do on the sales side, especially if the renter has kids who can go outside and play with a lesser chance of getting hit by a passing car. Also if the neighborhood is driven by amenities, make sure you look at its location to those amenities and ease of access.

Age of the House

Some neighborhoods have phases. I have seen many that have much smaller houses in the second phase, and the older homes are larger and of nicer caliber. Make sure you are not dealing with a multiyear-developed area and that your comparison properties have a similar year, builder, and location.

Number of Bedrooms and Bathrooms

As a rough estimate, an additional bedroom (make sure it's a livable bedroom) adds about $100 to $150 a month more to your property's rental value. But they need to have the appropriate number of bathrooms. A five-bedroom house with only two full bathrooms does not add much—except obvious frustration to the renter.

Days on the Market

The number one indicator of a price that is too high or too low is the numbers of days a property sits on the market. Remember earlier when I talked about the experience of getting the deal? This is where dollars and cents actually make sense. If you have a rental in a hot area that rents in a couple of hours, and every other house in the area rents in a couple of hours, you need to evaluate your rental number. You may want to put an additional $50 to $100 a month on that property and watch the trends for renewal increases. Or if you have a great property that takes 120 days to rent, then you may want to evaluate the rental amount checking for earlier parameters and characteristics that could be a little off.

Let's say you are putting your house up for rent in December, and all of the other comparisons you have predict the house sitting empty for over sixty days. (It should be thirty days or less.) Well, check out the time of year and make sure it's not the holidays. This is where the "deal" happens. Offer a discount if the home is rented by X date and run that special for three months. Sticking to your guns in this scenario can easily cause you to lose more money than if you do a discount even for the next year. When my friend's wife drives across town to save $0.10 per gallon on gas, we call that "running over dollars to pick up dimes." Use dollars and sense to your advantage. Know the prime seasons and adjust as needed or offer incentives to make that move worth it even in the off season.

Appearance

OK, now it's time to get to the real influencer of rent. This is no surprise to you, so I am just going to rip right into it. Appearance is where most investors and rental prices hit the most snags. When you compare homes, look at pictures if they are available and see what type of condition the homes are in and what upgrades have been made. This could cause you to raise or lower your rent. Many people forget that every renter wants to feel like a homeowner and, for the most part, will treat the home better if it's in better condition to start with, although there are exceptions.

If the upgrades are made and the home has some updated features, you can overcome many obstacles. However, you need to match that appearance to your target age group. Don't believe for one second that the wallpaper with frogs on the pond and squirrels eating nuts will appeal to a young couple. Paint is cheap. You will get your money out of paint, and price will always be reflective of your insights into the right changes. Don't over-improve either. Make sure when you set the budget that you don't blow a wad of cash that leaves you with a huge payback period. Balance the "must haves" with the "nice to haves." Sometimes it may be better to charge a little less rent and not do the improvements.

A word of caution though: *remember from the last chapter to never let tenants perform improvements for a discount on the rent.* This is a lose-lose situation. They think they can paint or repair, but for every yes and every time I tried this early on, I got burned. The work, if ever done at all, was shoddy, cheap, and not as we agreed, so don't even do it.

Two Story versus One Story

If the neighborhood has primarily two-story homes, then follow the two-story trends in your pricing. But if your property is a ranch home interspersed in a two-story neighborhood, it's not an oddball; it's a benefit. Some families are drawn to two-story homes based on their age. But it's a fact of life that a ranch home or bedroom-downstairs home is a real benefit. Most investors are drawn to one-level homes or bedroom-down homes since the demographic trends older, making ranch homes open to more potential renters. Ranches command a higher rent by at least 5 to 10 percent compared to similar two-story homes of the same size and makeup. They are more expensive to build as the price per square foot brings more at retail.

Garages

Garages are typically more valuable than not, especially if the neighborhood does not have many. Recently, I helped a client buy a ranch home with a detached two-car garage in a neighborhood that did not have many garages. Now we have a gem worth at least 10 percent more than the base rent in the area. Tenants, like many of us, typically have more stuff than they have room. It is funny—older couples who rent have usually been homeowners and are also paying rent on a storage unit for things they just can't let go. You hear that so many times from people who are excited about having their car in the garage, but they are overcome by stuff, and the car sits outside in the sun anyway.

Schools and Area Amenities

Because of fair housing rules, Realtors® aren't permitted to talk about good versus bad schools in a given area. But the information and school ratings are available for all of us to look at. School demand and ratings can have a significant impact on rental prices. Rental areas with strong school ratings may bring 15 to 20 percent higher rental rates.

When you purchase a home with strong schools, the largest segment of the potential tenant population is looking to start renting between March and July. This is when you get your strongest pricing as the majority of parents don't pull their kids out of schools for a move until then. Of course, there are rare exceptions for those moving into the area, but we are talking about the typical moves.

Most corporate relocations happen during the first quarter of every year. If you have an executive-style home, you can demand a higher rent number during those months. If you do short-term rentals, those are typically your hottest month, so increase your rental amount by at least 10 percent January through March for short-term stays. In the fall through the end of the year, do the opposite: drop it by 10 percent.

Set the Price

Psychological pricing is alive and well! Use it. If your rental amount is $1,000, use $998. If your rental amount is $1,150 use $1,148. Many have argued that if someone is searching for rent between $1,000 and $1,500, it won't matter. I see some merit in that argument, but I can't tell you the number of times we have changed rent to the "8" pricing and gotten a renter immediately. Try it for yourself. If it works for Walmart, it works for me. Everyone wants a "deal" even if it just *appears* to be one.

Using all we've talked about already, come up with a base price for rent. Let's say for this example it's $998 ($1,000). Now, know the competition. If the other homes in the area rented in under fifteen days, then raise your rent to $1,098 ($1,100), an increase of 10 percent. Or for much lower rent ranges, increase it by $50 or 5 to 6 percent.

Look at the time of year. If you are renting a home in a hot school area in December, run a special that says if you rent the home by the end of December, you will offer a Christmas special for the next three months of $900 or a gift card for the same amount of savings if they pay the rent for all three months on time.

If the home has sat past thirty days, change the price. If you are getting tons of applications and the price is not the issue, then it could be:

- You need to suck it up and just wait for the right applicant and hold your price. We had one home that had thirty-seven applications, but we did not rent it until we had the right one.

- Your price is just too low. Increase it to end in a $98 or $48 and see what happens.
- You need to fix something about the home that does not match the demographic you are after. Learn from my mistake here: I built a brand-new home for rental in a very hot area—walkable streets, farmers market, cool shops, and two taverns nearby to attract a mid-thirties audience. I missed a small thing that audience wanted: smart home devices. I got smart and made the house smart with a lock, two lights on the front porch, and a thermostat that could be operated with a smartphone. It rented immediately after that.
- You need to advertise it with more than just a sign. Go to the paid rental sites and pay for the advertising. Do not use just the free sites—you will get scammed. You have to watch for that anyway. This is another argument for using a Realtor® or a management company to help you control your property data better.

If the tenant wants a deal upfront before they apply, do not negotiate rent until you pull their credit and background check. Let's say you set your rent at $1,498, and a tenant comes along and says they will give you $100 less and will move in tomorrow. Warning, Dr. Smith! (Not everyone will get that quote, but some *will*.) When a tenant wants an upfront deal like that, you usually find a credit issue. Here is what you say: "We can discuss the rental amount once I have received and reviewed your full application."

A Word on Annual Increases

If you raise your rent annually, they will not move out. Even a small increase every year is a must. Investors always say they are afraid tenants will move out. Just remember that it costs to move—they are not going to move due to a small increase. If they were living in an apartment, they could expect an increase every year there too. I know in your head you're thinking you don't want to rock the boat. But your costs are going up—if you don't raise the rent, you lose on your returns.

Many tenants are going to move whether you raise the rent or not. If it's a big increase and they move, *do the math.* If rent needs to go up substantially, it may be better that they do move out. Say goodbye and get a new tenant.

Establish the Rent
Key Takeaways

Research your rent comparables, meaning compare your property to similar rental properties. Be clear on the differences like condition and location and neighborhood phases.

When looking at comparable rents, don't be fooled by high rates when the comparisons you use have been on the market for a long time.

Know your audience (potential tenants). Be clear about who they are and what they want or care about.

Notes

A lease is a **covenant between a landlord and a tenant** for a specific term and specific amount of money with very specific guidelines.

CHAPTER 6

Write the Lease

I got a call from a tenant who was with me for three months. Last we saw her, she loved the home, and other than a few small repairs, she was a raving fan. She paid her rent on time, and the moon and stars were aligned, bringing the owner a great return.

As it turned out, she had a better place in mind and decided she wanted to move out. We explained to her that, yes, she could move out, but she was responsible for the rent until such time that we found a replacement tenant. Oh man, the mood took on a new tone. She explained that she no longer felt safe, didn't like the electric panel being outside, and that she was going to hire a lawyer—oh, and of course call the North Carolina Real Estate Commission and complain. (It gets more interesting: we were fine with her filing the complaint in North Carolina because the house was actually in South Carolina.)

Honestly, we all know what is happening here. I get it every so often when folks sign a covenant (lease) and then decide something different. However, it's a little different than returning a coat to the department store or part of a twelve-pack back to Costco. It impacts everyone and even the home itself. The quick in and out gives the impression of a problem, and the house gets the stink eye (the perception of bad things happening).

To continue the saga, she harassed my people and did call the real estate commission and file a complaint (yes, in the wrong state). Then she did pay, and we did find a new tenant. But funny story—being the great person she claimed to be, she tried to bring in a replacement tenant who turned out to have a 450 credit score and animals galore. Geez, that's the kind of help you don't want to have.

The morale of this story: get a good, solid lease and know how to handle what comes your way. Also know this: tenants know the law, and they know the lease. If there is a loophole, they know it or will work to find it. Threats are an unfortunate weapon against personal responsibility, so expect it.

Your lease is the covenant and ruling document between you and the tenant on how the parties are to behave (or not) during the time of tenancy, including the rental rate, but honestly it's so much more than that. This document is really the key to whether you have a leg to stand on or you lose an arm and a leg. And I wish I didn't have to say this, but I will—even if you're leasing to family or a friend, they still have to sign a lease. Your lease needs to be lock-tight. Don't think for a second a self-made written lease will not be challenged.

What a Lease IS NOT

It is *not verbal*. I don't know how many times I've wished that a handshake was truly a bond between people in all forms of agreements. I remember my father telling me a story that my grandfather would make agreements with a handshake and that he was always well respected because everyone knew if he said he would do something, they could set their watch by it. My grandfather could not really read or write; he barely knew how to sign his name. But he knew—as his father before him, who was a blacksmith—in order to get along in the country, your word was your bond and meant something. If it did not, you would very quickly fail yourself and your family, and the disgrace of that act would be felt for generations.

It saddens me that today there seems to be no real concern or self-responsibility for what people say or commit to verbally. I was always taught to let your *yes* be *yes* and your *no* be *no*. I try and live based on the ways of my grandfather and know many who do. Even so, I look to nonverbal, written agreements as the only true way to protect myself and my family in just about anything having a clear impact on our finances and future liability.

If you ask an attorney, they will tell you that verbal contracts may or may not have merit. But let's face it—they are tough to deal with, so why risk it?

What a Lease IS

There are many forms of leases. Some have short-term provisions and are tailored for daily, weekly, or monthly tenancy, and others have much longer terms. Commercial and residential leases are also very different. For our purposes, we will focus on residential leases. In North Carolina and South Carolina where I practice, I use the forms available to me as an agent from the North Carolina Real Estate Commission—approved forms that are written by attorneys and have passed the "sniff test" of defensible for terms that carry the most weight if ever there were to be a dispute. Of course, they do not cover absolutely every situation, but they do a great job of giving you some parameters. *Let me say again, I caution you not to write your own lease agreement even though it is legal to do so.*

Several years ago, I had a lease for an office building I rented that was two pages of bulleted points that basically said, "You will pay on time or leave. You will not damage my place, or I will come after you. You will not sue me, and I won't sue you. We will act civil and settle all disputes like adults." And this lease lasts for three years. I will never forget it. It was back in the 1990s, and the owner of the building could not stand attorneys, so he wrote his own lease. It had fourteen bullet points, and we both signed it.

Sample Components of a Lease

A lease is a covenant between a landlord and a tenant for a specific term and specific amount of money with very specific guidelines. Many provisions in the lease truly must be there. You can search for samples online. You can obtain a lease from many sources. A local agent would be the best source. The National Association of Independent Landlords (NAIL) is another.

Long story short, below is a list of information included in a lease:

1. The full, legal names of parties involved, including the landlord (owner) and tenant (renter).
2. The address of the property.
3. Who is allowed to stay there, including specifications about the tenant's children, parents, and other relatives, and how long guests are allowed to stay before they must be included on the lease.
4. Whether the property allows pets and any rules involving said pets. (We use an addendum to outline our pet policy.)
5. What happens if rent is late and whether additional fees apply to late payments.
6. Terms of the lease (how long it lasts) and what happens at the end of that term.
7. What the tenant is responsible for, such as paying rent, following HOA rules, keeping utilities on, being a good neighbor, and/or not destroying the place.
8. What the landlord is responsible for, such as meeting building codes, making repairs when necessary and in a reasonable time, and/or keep the premises safe.
9. Who pays which expenses, such as utilities, garbage, alarm, lawn care, etc.
10. When the owner can enter and what notice is required.
11. Whether the property is part of an HOA and, if so, what rules must be followed and who the contact is.
12. What happens when damage occurs.

13. What changes are allowed to the property, such as hanging curtains, painting interiors, hanging pictures, and whether such changes require written permission.
14. What constitutes a breach.
15. What happens when rent isn't paid and how the notice process works.
16. How things end (termination) on both parts.
17. Requirements and terms for the tenant to carry renter's insurance.
18. How and when inspections are performed.
19. Appropriate ways for notifications to be delivered.
20. Where to sign, date, and initial every page.

Again, this list is not meant to take the place of a lease—it's just twenty things that should be a part of any lease to set up good communications between the landlord and tenant. The one we use is eight pages and contains many other provisions. I don't want to drill down too far into the weeds, but I think you get the point that the lease must be in writing and executed (signed and dated), and all parties should have a copy. Check the rules of your state for any other provisions that may be considered important.

Who Is on the Lease Matters

A common misconception: when you have multiple roommates on a lease and one moves out, the person who is leaving feels they are no longer obligated for that lease. Nay, nay. They are on the lease and will remain on it until it is revised and initialed by all parties or a new lease is drafted with the remaining roommates or new tenants. Make sure all roommates understand their responsibility. With almost every three-plus-roommate situation I have leased to, this misconception has been a problem. They have a break up, or someone gets married or changes jobs. We had one situation where one roommate brought in a dog, and even though the dog did not belong to all the roommates, the responsibility for pet damage was shared equally by all roommates.

Short-Term and Vacation Rentals

I use a lease even for short-term and vacation rentals. For the most part, the same provisions apply, except that we use deposits for damage and have provisions with clear language around liability in the event they trip, fall, or crash a bike or cart we may use. Another reason to use leases in these types of rentals is for hold-over provisions (the renter not leaving). We have clear language as to when they are approved to enter and when they are to leave. The more initials you get on each of those paragraphs, the better. That says they read each one or at least acted like it. Have an attorney look your lease over carefully, or as we discussed, get an attorney-approved lease.

Addendums and Their Evolution

This is where you will really learn by fire. I thought that the terms and provisions in an eight-page lease would be more than ample for any situation and any tenant and surely enough protection for all the challenges we would face. That would be a huge NO.

Even today, I am facing the evolution of more and more addendums to add to the lease. Note that in order to be effective, addendums must be identified in the main lease, and each one must be signed and dated. Just handing a tenant the sheet with "provisions and rules" means nothing. It must be a part of the master covenant between landlord and tenant. So let's talk about the evolution of a few addendums we have in place now.

Nonsmoking

If you give an inch on these rules or aren't clear, you'll have a problem. The addendum must cover any and all smoking products and lay out clear instructions about the house being a nonsmoking house. It must also be clear about damages and fees the tenant will face if the policy is violated. I don't know if you have ever been in the house of a smoker, but the smell gets in everything and must be professionally remediated, and all fabric surface materials that are affected must be replaced. Having to repaint is common, and many homes need more than one coat. You can't just paint the room affected; it typically takes repainting every wall in every room.

It's funny that you have to go such detail of making the house nonsmoking, not just the person. I had a renter who was a nonsmoker, but they had a guest who was a smoker and didn't prohibit the guest from smoking in the house since they, as the tenant, were the only ones obligated not to smoke. So make sure your nonsmoking addendum is broad and encompassing.

Drugs and Other Illegal Activity

You would think illegal activity would be an obvious nonstarter in a rental. Well, think again. You could be held liable for any illegal activity that happens on your property, yet a tenant breaking the law is not a legal reason you can evict them unless you have provisions for just that in your lease. Cannabis use, in particular, is tricky since it is now legal in some states. But smoking cannabis can leave similar odors and stains as smoking tobacco. In a multifamily building, it becomes even more of an issue that is "high" on the priority list of things that some tenants would complain about. Note that you do have to catch tenants violating this policy; you cannot rely on hearsay to make this claim. Other things might include production of methamphetamines inside the home or even operating a business out of the home that is not zoned for business, like a daycare that is not licensed or a business that is not approved by zoning or a city ordinance.

Bedbugs

Bedbugs, although eradicated years ago, are now back on our soil. Travelers that venture abroad have given them back to us, and they are some sneaky little bugs—nearly undetectable until you have an active infestation. Many high-end hotels are known to be among the largest culprits. It's best to keep your luggage in the tub or wet areas and far away from your bed when you return home. Do your research—it's a big deal. So once you find them in your home, you must treat them to make them go away, it's not easy and for sure not cheap either. We are in the process now of adapting our addendum to further clarify that no bed bugs were present when the tenant moved in, so if bugs do come, the tenant owns the issue fully. Without an addendum covering bedbugs, the tenant could bring them in, and if they prove they have an infestation, you would be forced to remediate the problem, and the tenant could use it to break their lease. It's a loaded issue, and remediation of bedbugs is truly going to affect your return on investment at any price point as the average remediation can run from $1,500 to over $10,000 depending on the extent of the infestation.

Spices

Yes, you are reading this right. Spices can affect a home in some ways as bad or worse than smoke can. This addendum is one of my more recent additions. It came about when a tenant who enjoyed cooking with spices did it in a brand-new townhome. When they moved out of the property, on the surface it was in pristine condition—except the smell. Curry was the spice of choice for this tenant, and there were others, but the townhome absolutely reeked of curry, and there was no air freshener in the world that was going to mask it. I found a company that specialized in chlorine treatments to remediate these types of things. If you work with one of these companies, make sure they guarantee their work. Turning on the HVAC can stir up the stink. Thankfully, the home is now odor free, but it took two treatments at a cost of $1,400.

Pets

Yes, it does happen. A tenant brought a pet into one of my houses without authorization. I did an inspection, and when I found the dog, they explained how great it was. Then as timing would have it, the dog made a mess on the carpet. Yes, the dog and tenant are both gone.

Having a pet policy does not mean you hate pets; it means you want to have a say in and knowledge of the animals entering your investment property and the rules for doing so. If the original lease says they may have no pets or it tells you the limit of the number of pets allowed, then you must follow that path consistently and enforce the rules without exception. So here are the important aspects to a pet policy and addendum:

- A clear yes or no to whether pets are allowed.
- What types of pets are allowed (cats, dogs, only one or the other, etc.).
- How many pets are allowed.
- Breed restrictions. (Typically, you get this from your insurance company.)
- What happens if they bring in a pet that is not approved, e.g., it must be removed in forty-eight hours.
- How to apply for approval of a pet.

"Support and service animals" are a big part of peoples' lives these days. We recently had someone submit an application for two big dogs. Well, the owner and I agreed that two big dogs would tear the daylights out of their house, and the owner's policy was clear that acceptance of a pet was at the owner's discretion. So we denied the application. Then the prospective tenant went online and got a support animal certificate that they paid $40 for and resubmitted their lease application. We went to the Americans with Disabilities Act (ada.gov) and Fair Housing Act (hud.gov) websites to search for approved animal certifications, and the prospective tenant's certificate obviously was not on the list. Then they were denied a second time.

Make sure you know the rules because in many cases, you cannot deny a family the right to a support animal. Here are a few websites with helpful information:

- National Service Animal Registry (nsarco.com/emotional-support-animal-housing.html)
- ADA National Network (adata.org/learn-about-ada)
- US Department of Housing and Urban Development (www.hud.gov/sites/documents/SERVANIMALS_NTCFHEO2013-01.PDF)

These are just for reference, so do your own careful research. You can bet even if you don't know the rules, they do. Don't trip yourself up.

Here is a great example. I had a woman who applied to rent a unit from us. She worked with my new, very green property manager. My staff member told the disabled (deaf) tenant that the unit was not approved for a pet, and if it was, a deposit was required. Do you think I was on the phone quickly to get that fixed? You are darn right I was, and that tenant was with me for five years, and the dog was too.

Social Media

I bet you can't wait to hear about this one. Yes, it's viable now to guard your company, yourself, your family, and your investment from social media woes. Many times, a very "needy" tenant does not understand the meaning of the word "emergency" or "not a new house" or that a light bulb being out is their own issue. It is common, even with the best communication, that you as an owner or property manager or agent can be absolutely slammed on social media for any and all reasons with no recourse.

I once got attacked on social media for holding back part of a security deposit from someone who absolutely had damaged a part of a home. He then proceeded to go to every venue to complain—Facebook, Yelp, Twitter, Better Business Bureau, and the real estate commission. It was clear, documented damage. However, I did not have a social media addendum in place, so I was defenseless against his one-sided claim. It was a very powerful lesson to me, a baby boomer who puts no credence in social media, that I better start. Now this is a very important part of our lease to protect us and our owners from such personal attacks against our reputation.

Maintenance

You must outline who is responsible for what types of maintenance. If it is not in the main lease, you need to protect yourself from the "pay and pester" tenant. It is just the funniest thing when we get maintenance tickets for cleaning items and disposables like light bulbs, batteries, and filters. Our lease clearly spells out who does what and who pays. It also requires them to do a few other things—drip faucets during freezing weather, clean gutters, rake leaves, and in some cases, trim shrubs once a year. If you *don't* want them to do something, spell that out as well.

Human nature tells us that if you don't include something, they won't even consider doing it—just like my teenagers. I saw a commercial where parents left their son a list of how to do laundry, and when the parents confronted him about why the clothes were not folded after he washed them according to the instructions, he said it wasn't on the list. They then proceeded to text him—it made me chuckle. If it's not on the list, guess who's doing it? You! New examples and lessons will always arise.

Executing the Lease and Any Changes

I am not an attorney, but I do know that it is not a valid lease until it is fully "executed," meaning signed and dated by both parties with copies of the signed document(s) for each party. In some states, it also has to be witnessed. I have had some tenants say they never got a signed copy. Many property owners forget this step. It must be given to them *signed*. It can be delivered by email, mail, in person, or to their leasing agent. In fact, our system automatically gives them a copy. It doesn't matter if they can't find it. If you can track and confirm that it was transmitted, you are all set.

Some people also record the lease at the courthouse. Some banks require this, and in some places, it is considered an extra layer of protection. We don't do that. Check with your attorney for the best path for you in your state.

If you make changes, they must be in writing and also initialed unless your lease has provisions allowing notification without approval, like changing banks for their security deposit or automatic renewals of leases.

Keep your executed leases on file for seven years after the lease expires. If you put an arrangement in an email, keep record of it printed out in the file as well. Our lease files also used to contain some personal information on the tenant, so we have secured that information behind locked doors and in a locked cabinet to protect us all. Any digital information needs to be stored in a secure cloud environment.

Write the Lease
Key Takeaways

A fully executed lease is a legally binding document that sets expectations for both tenant and landlord behavior. Since you get to choose your lease, it should favor you. If they don't want to sign it, they don't get to move in.

Addendums that outline additional rules and expectations must be referenced in the lease and also signed and dated.

Don't go on the cheap and copy someone else's lease, and unless you are an attorney, don't write your own.

Notes

Tenant screening is not
a perfect science, but it
can give you a picture of
**who prospective tenants
are and how they live.**

CHAPTER 7

Screen Tenants

When it comes to tenant screening, everyone asks the same question or makes the same statement. It's not just how to screen for tenants effectively but also how to screen for a tenant that pays on time or early, treats the house like they own it, makes their bed every morning, does not complain, has no pets, and basically never does anything that causes any waves at all. We call it the "invisible tenant." Who wouldn't want that kind of tenant? Who wouldn't want a tenant who just sends your check—early mind you—never says a word, fixes any little issues on their own, and has the pride of ownership in the rental to keep it like it is their own?

But we are dealing with the human condition here. People are still people at the end of the day, and what was once invisible can become visible at a moment's notice. People lose their jobs; they break up; they get mad. People we think are great in the beginning one day have an issue that turns them into the tenant from you-know-where. They want you to change their light bulbs or handle other minor issues, and tenant screening does not see this in them. But it does sometimes see trends and signals you can pick up on.

Tenant screening is not a perfect science, but it can give you a picture of who prospective tenants are and how they live. Sounds like a job interview, right? Well, in essence it is. And the tenants know it. If you were about to hand over the keys of your brand-new car to a complete stranger to use daily for an extended period of time, wouldn't you want to know a few things? Yes, screening is an art, but just like art, it has imperfections that you may or may not be able to see. In this chapter we will talk about those things.

Too Good to be True

Let's say we have a property manager who loves everyone. When she meets a family to show a house, she always wants to rent to everyone even if their background looks awful. Her personality focuses on the emotional attachment they show for the house. But their behavior during the showing process is just as critical as the first interview for a job. This reminds me of a one-of-a-kind story we faced that is almost too much to believe, and we have never had anything like it ever happen again, so just know that you can't see everything in a tenant background screening.

We had a couple with four children approach us for a showing in South Charlotte. They were clean, drove a nice car, and were courteous to a fault. After the wife's preview, they came to the office to get more details and apply. The property manager at the time agreed to ride over to the house for one last quick look as the husband had just gotten into town, and they needed a place to stay—right away, no delay. They were moving to Charlotte, and the movers had all of their possessions in a truck awaiting a place to unload.

We then proceeded to perform the normal screenings—verifications and background and credit checks. The tenant was self-employed, so we gathered tax returns and bank statements to make a credit decision. The tenant then agreed to pay one year's rent upfront and a double security deposit to cover a pet that was older and of the approved breed. Once everything was verified, we did our other final checks, and everything seemed in order. They moved in, the transition was smooth, and certified funds were deposited into the appropriate trust accounts well before turning over the keys to the rental home.

It was a Friday night when my cell phone rang. A gentleman from the Atlanta office of the FBI asked me if I knew a Mr. So-and-So and where he was at that moment. I asked him how I would know he was for real, and he said, "No problem. I will fax you something."

"Sure," I said, "fax me something. Thank you very much, but no thanks. If you want to prove who you are, then I want the chief of police from the town of Matthews to call me on my cell phone and tell me it's OK for me to share this info with you. That's on top of the subpoena that you supposedly are going to 'fax' to me."

He said, "No problem," and we hung up.

I thought, how naïve must this guy think I am? I didn't give it another thought and went about my business of working on audits and other busy work you want to get out of the way at the end of the week.

Then my cell phone rang again. It was Chief Hunter from the Matthews Police Department. Oh, crap. You can guess what happened next. Chief Hunter made it very clear that they weren't messing around and I needed to give up what I knew right then. It wasn't the Russians or a scam from some other evil doers in another country—it was indeed the real FBI.

After a quick call, the FBI went to the house and arrested the husband for a variety of charges. Not only that, the FBI also had me return all of the money the tenant ever paid to us and the owner. Yes, they did give us some of it back, but how in the heck do you explain to an owner that the FBI wants the money back now and the tenant we put in the house is a suspected felon?

Well, here's the note to remember in this absolute extreme case: in this country, you are innocent until proven guilty. Nothing showed up on his records because he had not been found guilty of anything. He'd been charged but was not a part of a formal public crime database nationally or otherwise. No one would have known. It's not a perfect science. No clues presented themselves except one: we no longer accept one year of rent up front. In many cases, that is a sign of trouble; when a tenant offers that, it raises a red flag that reminds us we are always learning.

The "art" of screening is a never-ending teacher of the human condition, and just when you think you have seen it all, heard it all, and dealt with it all, you are always proven wrong.

What to Look For

Remember when I started this chapter, I talked about the property manager who loves everyone? Having a kind, warm, and gregarious agent is always good. People feel comfortable quickly, which can be a real asset in the right circumstances. We want to attract good tenants—people who are qualified, good natured, and likable—because when problems happen, and inevitably they can, you want to know who you are dealing with. You also need a degree of understanding that sometimes things happen that people just can't control.

We do, however, look for tell-tale signs. Obviously, some of these signs are subtle, but we look at them just the same. As we will discuss later, it is not a matter of prejudice or any kind of discrimination; it's a matter of whether the prospective tenant's words match what we see later in various screening data and employer records.

An applicant once told me that her son would be moving into the home in thirteen months. It seemed like an odd number, so I asked his age. He was nineteen. Then I asked her if he was in prison. Sure enough, he was. Questions must be asked. Even the most-simple questions can reveal information that make your decision easy.

People who are up front about everything, even if the news is bad, deserve at least a look before you determine their eligibility. Many of us have had issues in our lives we couldn't control. It's how we handle ourselves and how we move forward that gives a glimpse of who we are today and how we handle life in general. Again, you have to ask the questions.

Back to pets as an example. When we ask applicants if they have a pet, if they say no, we then ask if they are planning on getting one. If they do have one, what breed is it? Most of the time when they say "terrier," it's a pit bull, and we do not accept certain breeds as a policy. Get that list of breeds from your insurance company and apply it consistently.

As I mentioned earlier, another thing to look for is if they are negotiating your rental amount up front. If they are, it may be because they want to negotiate before you see their credit score or history. In a market as dynamic as ours, the rental market is very competitive. We sometimes change the rent, but it is related to a sliding scale of increases over a longer term with a clear owner-out clause with proper notification, and we do not like leases any longer than two years. So watch for hard negotiations up front; it's usually a sign they have a blemish that concerns them.

Really, that full disclosure I spoke of earlier is the signal that they could be a truly good tenant. They may have either faced rejections and know you are going to find out, or they really are making good strides in their lives and want to continue moving forward in a more positive way. Honor them with at least a look, but still make a business decision based on the facts, and steer clear of anything in the process that might look like discrimination. That is a slippery slope, so dot your I's and cross your T's.

Also ask questions like, why are you leaving your current home, house, or apartment? If they mention the need for more room, closer to work, or a job change, these comments can easily be verified. A quick line of follow up questions can also bring things to light. How big is your current place? What will a larger place help you achieve? If they say because their parents are moving in or they want a dog or they're getting married, then that tells you what you need to know. A job change excuse is a signal to verify later. But if they launch into a litany of complaints about the current landlord, how bad they cared for the place, the things that went wrong, complain, complain, complain, take note because you may be next, and chances are you will be. Sure, there are some crappy places out there, so get the address. Google Street View it and even drive by. Take a look at the way it's kept. Call the previous landlord to verify some of the prospective tenant's facts. Again, it will tell you a ton. Also, is their car full of garbage and not cared for? That's certainly not a full signal for denial, but it shows a trend of carelessness. Let's face it—what you see is more often that not what you get. It sounds like stalking, but it's not. Bottom line: are they who they say they are, and are they acting the way they say they do?

Getting the Facts

Let's get down to what is available. These facts are the basis of the application that makes the business of tenant screening an art. It's not the parts but the sum of the parts that makes this a go/no-go scenario.

The Application

Remember that the application has to be the same process for all. It does not matter if you know them or they are friends of friends. It's a do-it-the-same-for-all scenario. You do not have the luxury today to let someone slide by without following this process. It's a slippery slope if you do that and grounds for discrimination, so be careful.

The application covers what you would expect it to cover: name, current address, occupants, pets, employment, income, personal data, criminal history, driver's license, pay stubs, and authorizations to access credit score and data and call upon all that is available. Remember that in order to access credit scores, you must have their permission. If you pull someone's credit without their authorization, it's a big deal. Make sure you have that in writing.

Also charge them something. If you don't ask for some form of a reasonable application fee, you give the impression that you may or may not actually be verifying this stuff. Charging for it also weeds out those who may know that denial is eminent. I get calls all the time with people who call and say, "I don't want to spend the money if you are going to deny me," or "Here is my situation; do I have a chance?" and "What criteria are you looking for?" We ask for three times the rent in income, no evictions, and no criminal activity of the sort that warrants immediate denial. These calls are great to get because they screen themselves out. Otherwise, they call and want their money back if they are denied by us. Seriously—it's amazing.

> We ask for three times the rent in income, no evictions, and no criminal activity of the sort that warrants immediate denial.

In our business, we require everyone over the age of eighteen living in the home for more than two weeks to apply. Anyone who moves in after tenancy must apply as well before they are approved.

Verify the Facts

Now you have the application, you have the picture, and you have done a national database search for evictions and criminal or sex offenses. You have pulled their credit and have the score; you see their total credit picture. You have their pay stubs, employer information, and list of places where they have lived. What do you do next?

I spent many years of my life owning and flying airplanes. I flew in all types of conditions and flew multiple types of private aircraft. One thing they taught you when you were flying was to trust your instruments. What that means is that in some situations, your body says you're flying level in the clouds, but the inner ear will lie to you. You could be completely upside down or on a 90-degree turn, and your body would not know the difference. The instruments, however, tell the truth. The application process is no different. Start the verification process by making the effort to validate the items you see and that are presented.

Put in the calls. Call the employer. Ask the following questions from the appropriate manager or HR department:

- Is this person employed there and for the number of years they stated?
- Is this person still making the same salary as the pay stub provided?
- Are they still eligible for continued employment?
- If so, do you see any reason why they would not be continually employed there?

Then, the big call: their past landlord. Sometimes you have to send a form. If it is a management company, send a form for them to fill out answering the following questions:

- Have they been late on rent?
- Would you rent to them again?
- What was the condition of the unit at last inspection?
- How long were they there?
- How much was the rent?
- Have they provided notification?
- Did they have pets? If so, how many and what breeds?
- Number of occupants?
- Share any additional comments.

It's always best though if you can get them on the phone. Someone may tell you something that they don't want to put in writing.

If the previous landlord is an individual, they may have a tendency to tell you more just because they don't know any better. That's fine. Just listen; you will learn a ton, especially if the applicant talked poorly about the landlord. Find out how they work with the landlord, how they communicate. Ask the same questions you would ask a company but continue to expand on things important to you and the tenancy. For example, if the applicant has a pet, how did the pet treat the house? Who is living there with them? What was the relationship like? Was that person they are living with a problem? When did they move in?

Then I want you to do something we do that will surprise you: go to the tax record for that address and match up the landlord name you were given with the person you are talking to. We have had multiple situations where we were given a fake landlord and found the real owner was not who we talked to. This is a critical step in the verification process. Don't skip it.

If there is a criminal record on the report, verify it was them. Sometimes we have found that common names cause criminal record mismatches. Ask the prospective tenant about it. You might also be able to access public criminal records to find a picture. Also know the law before you say no. Criminals have certain tenancy rights, but the law is vague, so be careful. We'll discuss that more in the following pages.

If the credit score is low or the credit report reveals something odd, ask the prospective tenant about it. People don't make a habit of checking their credit, and things may appear that are really not them. Things may also appear that drive down the score that you may want to ask about, or a charge for a crime may be on there from thirty years ago. Ask, verify, and take it all into consideration.

Regarding evictions, make sure the database you access is national, not just local to the state or county. This is very important to ensure you get the right data. When you tell applicants about the initial screening parameters, make sure they understand that any evictions within the last X years (number of years up to you) will result in immediate denial. And be consistent when applying that rule.

Check social media. People put things out there that you may not otherwise be able to see.

Lastly, I want to discuss a step that involves some subjectivity. It may seem like an overreach, but to us it has proven helpful. Check social media. People put things out there that you may not otherwise be able to see. But, hey, if they put it out there, look at it. It's another step to verification that they are who they say they are and have what they say they have. Live-in boyfriends, pets, habits, and pictures of their place can really tell a ton about them. You see people that visit, parties they may hold, attitudes about their current residence, and more. If they complain about their landlord or management company, or are just generally nasty and negative publicly, or have pets with them in a photo, or claim to have at least one, you can guess what's next. You're next. Don't think for a minute that their attitude and lifestyle won't move with them to their next place.

If you see anything else that seems odd, remember to always ask the applicant and then verify.

What Is Protected from Discrimination and What Is Not?

The federal Fair Housing Act rules are a big deal. Yes, it's your house and your investment, but if someone applies to live there, you cannot make a decision to rent it to them based on those parameters.

Protected Classes

The acronym FRESH CORN shares other parameters you cannot consider in your decision according to fair housing standards. Put this in your brain and don't let it go.

Note that excluding all applicants who have a criminal history may mean you disproportionately exclude minorities since they are convicted at a higher rate relative to the general population. So while you are allowed to have a criminal history policy in place (and it better be in writing!) to safeguard your other tenants and your property, you cannot deny applicants simply because they have a criminal record. The US Department of Housing and Urban Development (HUD) issued detailed guidelines in this regard, which you can find online. Even better, consult an attorney on specifics that apply to you. Generally speaking though, you must consider the type and severity of an offense and how long ago it occurred. For example, if someone was convicted of drug possession, denying them would be considered discriminatory. If they were convicted of manufacturing or distributing drugs, however, you can deny them but must apply that standard consistently to all applicants. Also note that an arrest is not the same as a conviction—innocent until proven guilty.

Look—fair housing is not to be fooled with. If you have issues with any of these things, hire a management company to help you or find a different investment. Our country offers these rights to all those who are here legally. Enough said.

You Can't Say NO to FRESH CORN

Familial status (including children)

Race

Ethnic background

Sex (or gender identity)

Handicap*

Color

Origin (as in country of)

Religion (you can't even ask)

Nationality

* You are not required to make a home accessible, but you are required to allow them to make the home accessible with the proper approvals and at their expense.

Reasons to Say NO

Income	The applicant's income does not meet the minimum requirements you consistently set. My company requires three times the monthly rent in verifiable income. If the applicant is self-employed, get two years of tax returns. That should give you a good picture. Also, make sure pay stubs are current. If you don't see a clear path to making the rent (such as no job, job loss, or job pending), then you can say no.
Eviction	This is a clear no. An eviction that has been filed for but not completed should show up in the late payments to the previous landlord—also a grounds for no.
Criminal Conviction	If the nature of the crime could put other tenants or your property at risk—such as drug dealing, rape, child molestation, assault and battery, and arson—and is "recent," you can say no. The law on this topic is vague. Please consult an attorney in your area for clarity.
Number of Occupants	Typical occupancy in most areas is two people per bedroom. You can state that the number of occupants does not match the home. Further, if you have a septic permit that allows only three bedrooms, even though the home has four bedrooms, occupancy must follow the permit or as the law provides in your area.
Pets	You can state "no pets," you can state "no cats," you can limit the number and size of pets, and you can limit the type of pets. You are also able to set parameters on pet deposits or fees. The difference is easy: a fee is non-refundable, and a deposit is not. I sometimes do both and split it so that they put more in and get some back for good pet behavior.

Age Restrictions	If your community is age restricted, your rental can be age restricted as well.
HOA Rules	If your community is part of an HOA, then your lease should state that the tenant must comply with HOA rules. If an applicant is unable to do so, that's grounds for denial. For example if the applicant has a work truck, but the HOA forbids parking such trucks in driveways or curbside, then that applicant can be denied. Or if the HOA dictates that all cars must be parked in the garage, and the applicant has three cars, then it's a big no. Give the tenant a copy of the HOA documents.
Credit Score	Yes, you can deny based on credit score, but set your parameters carefully. Don't just say, "It's low. Sorry, you don't qualify." When you check the credit, be careful not to be shortsighted. A few late $30 medical payments can cause a low score, but consideration may still be justified.
Order	We review applications in the order in which they are received and state that policy on our applications. If you approve #1, then all other applicants can be denied.
Other	A variety of exceptions for roommates and other considerations exist depending on where your property is located. So check the law to make sure a no is OK. For example, you don't have to accept subsidized tenants in many areas, but again check your local occupancy laws to confirm.

Let's get back to the pet thing for a minute. Nowadays, a segment of the population has "comfort animals." You must be careful with this issue. Our veterans come with very special needs. One very common need is a support animal. One of my agents did not understand how things worked, but I quickly fixed the situation, and the vet was a great tenant for many years. But comfort animals can be a slippery slope. If you establish an up-front no-pet policy for a legitimate reason such as allergies, you can certainly deny any animal. If a building or community has pet restrictions, you have to deal with them on how that is handled. But let's face it: a large population of folks really do need these animals for comfort and to calm down issues they may be having. It's the real deal. First, be aware. Second, get verification of the need and validate that it is a necessity for that prospect. Refer back to chapter 6 for valid certifications. And please, please don't deny them tenancy without doing your homework.

Surprise Additions

Sometimes you screen, verify facts, verify insurance, and get all the paperwork signed, and then they spring an animal or a roomie on you. Make sure your rules are clear about that up front—changes require a new application. They may fight you on it. Make sure that you clearly and consistently follow your process and that your lease is ironclad.

Can Bad Credit Make a Good Tenant?

Maybe. Look at the whole picture. Make the evaluation based on what you know and what you see. Let's just say you can see where someone had a short sale, filed bankruptcy, or had an isolated issue from their past that drove their credit downward. Or maybe they faced a medical challenge that they are working to overcome. It may cause you to think twice.

I like people, for example, who had a short sale versus a bankruptcy. Think about it: they didn't just hand it back to the bank; they did their best to try and pay back the bank. If you see they have a good history of recovery, then they could be a great tenant. We advise them that we report to the credit bureau, so their good behavior can be rewarded.

Can Good Credit Make a Bad Tenant?

Also a maybe. Again, look at the whole picture. If you have a good wage earner who also has credit cards, cars, revolving credit, and heavy debt, and then you calculate the debt service versus what they are making, you may see a red flag. The minute they get one financial hiccup, guess what is not going to get paid—their rent. I have seen it time and time again: people who make great money and should actually own a house instead of renting, but they just don't have the right debt ratios. That can be from circumstances within their control or outside of it, but the truth of the matter is that your property is an investment and must be treated as such. Yes, I have denied tenancy due to the amount of credit versus salary. It may sound like a mortgage evaluation, and it kind of is. Many of my owners do have mortgages. I want to make sure they make the payment on time from rent dollars received.

How to Say No: The "No" Protocol

We recently had someone walk through the door with a chip on her shoulder—she was loaded and ready. Her previous landlord was a jerk, and the home was moldy. She had evictions on her record; she was hit by a car, which impacted her credit; and she demanded we give her a break and rent to her, or she would call the real estate commission. We gave her the number and showed her the door. When they bully you unnecessarily, it's time to help them find another place to occupy. We did not have a house big enough for her attitude, and it's time in my life I can't get back. Some people just push and push and push themselves right out the door. But we still followed our "no" protocol.

Here is how the "no" protocol works. You can say no under the parameters we discussed, but it requires action when an actual application for the property has been submitted. You must send them a denial letter—the "Dear John letter" of real estate. It should be either mailed or emailed and include the following information:

- Date applied
- Their name
- Property address they applied for
- Reason for their denial
- Your name

If a prospective tenant filed an application with you—even if it's very obvious why they are denied as in the example of the angry applicant I mentioned previously—you still need to formally respond to them with the reason for their denial. Otherwise, you open yourself up to possible discrimination under the Fair Housing Act. Here is a sample letter.

Dear Mr. Smith,

You applied for 123 Main Street on June 7, 2018, for the purpose of rental tenancy. Your application was received, and we are not accepting your tenancy for the following reason: your verifiable income you provided does not meet the qualifications of three times the monthly rent [or insert other reason here].

Thank you,
John Doe, Property Manager

This letter should be short, sweet, and to the point. The more you say, the more you risk. Notice I didn't say, "If you want more details, call …" or "If you have questions, feel free to reach out …." Nope, I am not offering that. Write it, send it, and move forward to the next applicant. If you take their money and screen them, you owe them a letter. That's all. Plain and simple. As a practice, my company is careful not to take money from everyone that applies, only if we are truly screening them. If we don't run it, we don't owe them a letter.

Screening a tenant boils down to this: look at the whole picture and evaluate the pieces. Make the assessment but don't rush to approve. If you are in dire circumstances and can't make a mortgage payment without getting a tenant, that is one of the worst ways to make a tenancy decision. I always tell owners and investors that I may rent the home in a week, three weeks, or two months. It's not about the time it takes me; it's about the tenant I put in there. The owner and I both have to live with those tenants, and just because they can raise the money for the initial start doesn't mean they will be a long-term success. It's a big decision and a privilege to be on either side of the equation: to have a home that you can make money from and build wealth and to be a renter who qualifies to be in that rental home. It should be a blessing for both families, and it should always be treated with respect. It's a fact—one side cannot exist without the other.

Screen Tenants
Key Takeaways

Ask good questions, get all the facts, and verify them to create a complete picture of your applicants before making a decision.

Know the law and establish clear policies to avoid discrimination under the Fair Housing Act rules and FRESH CORN.

When you say no, follow the "no" protocol.

Notes

This is definitely
their happiest—the very
moment they are
**moving in and beginning
a new adventure.**

CHAPTER 8

Move Them In

You have done your due diligence. You have checked all the boxes. You have a signed lease. Now it's time to move them in. What you do next dictates how the relationship will be going forward and most importantly how it will end. Here are the move-in rules. *Do not deviate from them for any reason.*

Move-In Rules

Provide the new tenant with move-in instructions.

These instructions describe how the move-in works, when payments and deposits are due, when proof of insurance is required, who to contact in various situations, how to make requests online or by email, the proper procedure for those requests and reasonable response times, and other expectations and policies. See sample move-in instructions in the appendix and online. At a minimum, the document should include:

- Descriptions of what is an emergency and what is not
- Contact or online information and procedures for both emergency and non-emergency requests
- Contact information for utilities

- Any special cleaning instructions (such as materials to use)
- Instructions for cleaning and/or replacing air filters
- Description of your inspection policy
- A copy of the move-in inspection form
- Any other rules, policies, or procedures
  the tenant must be aware of

Utilities are such an important part of this process and can quickly put things on the road to unhappy. At least one in four tenants find themselves without utilities at move-in or just after move-in. Once we hand over the keys, we immediately call the utilities and let them know to turn off our account within forty-eight to seventy-two hours, depending if it's a weekday or weekend. This is *always* explained to the tenant, but some of them only hear the odd voice of the cartoon character Charlie Brown's teacher: "Woh woh woh woh." Then when the utilities are cut off, oh my, they have a fit.

To the tenants' credit, with everything else going on during a move, this one detail is easy to miss. So we remind them frequently. If you have one of those arrangements where the utilities default to you (the owner) so that utilities never get cut off, you will be paying for some of the utilities until the situation is rectified. It's hard to prorate bills, and after the initial whining, you'll end up not charging them—and then the entitlement attitude begins. So set utilities to turn off. Notify tenants in writing at least twice (in the lease and in the move-in instructions) and provide them the info on who to call. Then remind them again when you turn over the keys. Just figure that you may eat up to seventy-two hours of utilities. It's just a part of the cost of doing business.

Get the money, not just some of it, all of it.

And get it in certified funds or a money order and make copies for your records. Do not take a personal check for the initial deposits and first month's rent. Further, make sure the funds are separated: the security deposit in one payment and the rent (or prorated rent) in another. The security deposit should sit in a separate account labeled as "tenant security deposit" and kept separate from your funds. It is the property of the tenant. It is not rent money. It cannot even be dispersed without proper documentation; otherwise, you can get yourself in deep do-do. (Just sayin' because it's not your money; it's theirs.)

For the rent payment, you should have at least one full month of both the rent and prorated rent. For example, if they move in on the twenty-fifth, don't allow them to bring just five days of prorated rent and then pay regular rent at the beginning of the next month. Get one month and five days.

Get their renter's insurance certificate.

A renter's insurance policy is cheap, usually less than $200 per year, so insist that tenants have them. Make sure their policy has provisions to pay for a hotel if the home is damaged to a degree that makes it unlivable, such as from a storm or natural disaster. Make sure it has at least $100,000 of general liability and that medical payments and other provisions are there to cover appliances and, of course, their own possessions in the event of a theft, fire, or similar damage of any kind. Have the property manager and the owner named as additional insured and check on the annual renewal.

Put the keys in a safe place.

We use clearly visible lock boxes with combinations. Don't hide loose keys under the welcome mat. I've found that many tenants will hunt for the keys, and once they have the keys, you lose every bit of your leverage. Don't give them the keys until you've gone through the right steps and all conditions are met. Why? Because once they are in, they aren't leaving. If you let them in to put food in the fridge, they have already moved in. Once they are in, they fall under tenancy rules, and you'd have to evict them to get them out. This varies from state to state, of course, but for the most part the principle is the same—you can't just take the door off and throw all their junk in the front yard even if it feels like they deserve it.

Jane—we'll call her that to hide her identity—is one of my property managers. The incoming tenant said she left the money with her parents who were at the house, and all Jane had to do was pick it up. Jane just knew the tenant was telling the truth, so she gave the tenant the combination to the lockbox and said she would come by to pick up the check from the parents. Well, yes, the parents were there, and the house was full of boxes. Funny though, the *one thing* missing—even though every other possession on Earth was in the house within hours—was a check. I made Jane stalk that tenant for two weeks until we got the funds. I was about as angry as a bear.

This brings up an interesting point: this is a people business, and we are compassionate for people, but this is an investment as well. Setting clear parameters, communicating them consistently, and most importantly, applying them consistently protects your investment. Be compassionate but keep a short leash. *You will continue to hear me say, "You don't pay; you don't stay!"*

Perform a move-in inspection.

I want to make sure you put yourself in the best position personally and professionally. The courts will almost always side with the tenant because they are the "perceived victim of the evil landlord." So again I say, get your ducks in a row and document everything.

Check out our move-in inspection form in the appendix and online. (It is constantly updated.) We provide it to tenants with their move-in instructions. We require the form back within three days after move-in, and if necessary, we do our own move-in inspection on the fifth day per our lease. The written move-in instructions also state that failure to return the form within three days indicates their agreement that everything about the home is perfect and that there are no blemishes or issues.

The form with the accompanying pictures ultimately decides how damage will be assessed and how much of the security deposit is refunded when the tenant moves out. It has to be signed by both the tenant and the landlord. Review it carefully.

Start your move-in inspection outside. Take pictures of the front door area, all sides of the house, the mailbox, the driveway, and more importantly, the shrubs, beds, grass, and general condition of the exterior and patio areas. Make note of whether they are clean and well kept and note any of your possessions you've left behind for the tenant's use (such as a grill, a lawnmower, or outdoor furniture). If you can reach them with a camera, note that gutters are clean as well. Also make sure photos have dates on them when you save them to the file.

Inside, most of this is common sense, but you may get a few nuggets here that you didn't think of. Take photographs of the following and make any necessary notes on your form:

- Walls in each room.
- Flooring and most especially carpet condition.
- Ceilings, especially below bathrooms—if they overflow the tub or shower on the second floor, and it leaks into the ceiling of the first floor, they cannot say the stains were there before.
- Fireplace area—if you have a TV mount for a flat screen, you want to show the condition.
- Kitchen and appliances—note if they are clean and well kept.
- Air filters—take a picture of them being fresh.
- Garage—show that it's empty and the condition of the garage door both inside and out.
- Bathrooms and tubs—many people do not care well for showers and tubs and use abrasive cleaners that damage the finishes and ruin them. Make sure your photos are clear.
- Any damage—be sure document it. It looks bad if you don't. It tells a judge that you believe your house is perfect. The only time that may be true is if it's

new construction. Document it either way. If there
are nicks in the walls, make sure you note them.

- Condition of doors and behind doors.
- Colors—many times things will get painted without
  owner authorization. You need a record of colors in case
  you end up with a black or Clemson-orange bedroom.
  I see a lot of decals that say things like, "Kiss me before
  bedtime." They can ruin a room's paint job. Our lease
  states no holes in the wall or decals. There are tons of
  products to hang pictures that do not require a hole.
- Light fixtures and fans—nothing is worse than a broken fan.
  Even though it's cheap to fix, it's still about $150 after labor.

> Here is a great tip to detect warning
> signs: involve the neighbors. Tell
> them about who is moving in, the
> number of people, and whether
> they have pets, and give them your
> contact information. We give them a
> refrigerator magnet with our info on it.

As human nature would have it, people have hiccups in their lives.
I remember getting a call from a tenant's neighbor on a Sunday
morning telling me that all the furniture from the house was in the
front yard. Evidently, the couple had a huge fight. The next day the
husband was gone, and a truck had taken all of their things away.
We were never notified. If it wasn't for the neighbor, we would not
have been able to step in as we are just not there every day like the
neighbors are.

The other big thing we find all the time is people and pets moving
in without our knowledge. We do count occupants and look for
signs of pets during inspections, but the neighbors are great about
keeping us informed if any of that changes. I think some neighbors

may enjoy it a bit too much. They become like super sleuth detectives. I know they are probably just bored at home, but still it's worth having them as an extra set of eyes and ears.

HOAs are another reason to involve the neighbors. Think about this: yard care is a huge deal with HOAs, and that's good. It makes sure the community looks nice. If a tenant is not keeping up with lawn maintenance, neighbors will let you know, which keeps you from becoming an HOA target. Once you're on their list, you will be on it forever—they don't like tenants inherently anyway.

Move-In Opportunity

Tenants will be at their happiest three times in your relationship:

1. When they get approved and you send them notification that they are approved and set up the move-in process for them to follow.

2. When you turn over the keys to them. This is definitely their happiest—the very moment they are moving in and beginning a new adventure.

3. When they turn their keys in at move-out and before you've done the move-out inspection and sent them a list of zero damages.

Any other times in the relationship, they may be happy or mad, depending on their personalities. But if you want to develop a solid footing for positive personal connection, these are the times to do it. These are also the best times to ask for a review, either on Google, Yelp, or even their own social media with your company tagged or using a certain hashtag. You could even offer an incentive for doing so—perhaps a gift card or a year's worth of air filters.

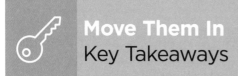

Move Them In
Key Takeaways

Provide move-in instructions in writing that explain the process and expectations.

Do not hand over keys until you have all the appropriate payments and proof of insurance.

Document the condition (including any blemishes) of the home at the time of move-in with both photos and written notes.

Notes

Documentation
is important

both for your sake
and the tenant's.

CHAPTER 9

Account for the Money

Just put the money in one big account. The software will figure it out. Yeah, right.

When I first bought a few rental houses, I lumped all the money together and gave them free rent for the last month, so I didn't have to refund their security deposits. I didn't know any better. Boy, did I learn quick. A tenant moved out and left a lot of damage—best I could tell he took a tire iron to the walls. I had no way of getting to him, and when I got the issue to court, the judge asked to see all my accounting, the lease, move-in reports, and inspections. I did not have all of those things handled correctly. And I never let that happen again.

Documentation is important both for your sake and the tenant's. Of course, our goal is to get rent payment from the tenant's hands into the owner's bank account as quickly and efficiently as possible, especially if there is a time sensitivity due to a mortgage payment. On the tenant's side, their goal is to get their security deposit back (always in full) as fast as possible. We know the harmony of money is always at work, so it may seem easier sometimes to melt everything together. But take heed—it's a trap if you do. Sometimes the extra steps can prove helpful for the owner and the tenant to avoid issues down the road.

This chapter talks about rules, regulations, and helpful hints of how money is handled at a very high level, along with some ways to protect the money from being mishandled. Note, however, that the rules and regulations we follow may not be the same for you. Also, when we handle money, we are not handling it from the property owner perspective. Although many of the same rules apply, we are working from a property manager perspective. So if you own your own property and also manage it, you really should consider treating it the same way with whatever changes your local rules require. Treat your rental property like a business because it is. You and the business are two separate things in the eyes of the IRS, even if it's just one house. I always tell people investment property is an annuity, and I am the fund manager.

Also note that this is not an accounting course, just some basic fundamentals to review. Get with a licensed agent in your state and a CPA to set things up right early or, like me early on, to fix it quickly. It's a common problem. When I take over a company or property from a landlord, it's the same time and time again: show me the money (trail).

Security Deposit

We talked about this a bit in the previous chapter, but it bears repeating. Let's establish a clear understanding of what that money is for and who owns it: the security deposit is the tenant's money held in trust to cover any damages discovered when they move out. It is not your money, and it is also not considered rent. It is the property of the tenant, held by you for security against damage or default.

Do not accept a combined check for the security deposit and first month's rent—keep them separate. Cash is the easiest to separate but the hardest to account for and have a record of. I always suggest that these funds come in an instant credit form: certified funds, money order, or wire transfer. If you really just want cash, give them a receipt and keep a copy for yourself. If they write a personal check that bounces after they move in, good luck trying to collect it after their stuff is in your house. We are real sticklers here: if they don't have it in the beginning, they will definitely not have it going forward.

Whichever form of payment you receive, document it. Make copies of checks, money orders, and cash receipts, and keep them on file for later reconciliation. Also make a copy of your deposit slip and attach it to the copy of the payment to confirm where and when funds were deposited.

It is imperative that the security deposit is put into an account that is not commingled with your personal funds or the funds where rent is applied. Again, ownership of security deposit funds resides with the tenant. Any time you use, take from, or reduce that amount, you must inform the tenant in writing, including where the money resides. I also recommend you name the account appropriately and make sure the account has the name "security deposit trust" or "tenant escrow account" to be sure it has a separate designation.

> I warn every owner never to use the security deposit as rent. It's a trap.

If you're a licensed real estate agent managing someone else's property, that account must be reconciled each month, and a reconciliation report must be on hand. If you manage your own property, you must still be sure to protect those funds and follow many of the same notification and account guidelines. If you spend that money or apply it to rent— don't do that!—then you are at risk for many issues. I warn every owner never to use the security deposit as rent. It's a trap.

Rent Payments

Everyone has a different way they want to handle collecting rent. Money comes into your hands in many forms. Some landlords give deposit slips to tenants and have them deposit money directly into the bank. For the right relationship, that may work, but I don't recommend it. It's not giving you any kind of record of payment other than the deposit you see on your bank statement.

My least favorite way is to visit the tenant to collect—yuck—unless they are disabled or elderly or otherwise physically unable to use a computer or drop off a check. Picking up the rent strips them of the responsibility, it's not fun to knock on doors, and it costs me too much money. If they have a smartphone, they can pay the rent electronically through sources like PayPal, Venmo, etc. If I do their work, then I get the next round of excuses, and I just don't have time for that any longer. I admit it—I did pick up rent in some cases; then they expected me to show up every time. But you know, I had a tenant who was blind but still got his rent to me on time on his own. Don't be a courier unless you have to. If a gentleman who is blind can pay me online, anyone can.

We also don't take cash unless absolutely necessary. We prefer direct deposit. Funds come in nicely recorded and buttoned up. We will take personal checks for proven tenants, and money orders also work like certified funds or cash. If you do take cash, realize that if you take money off the top of the rent, your deposit will no longer reconcile, and your tenant ledger will be skewed. Put it in the bank first, then take all you want.

Rent money should flow into a rental trust account (see illustration) as a whole amount and not be commingled with your security deposits or personal account. This keeps what's theirs theirs and what's yours yours. Then from that account, you can move the money forward for disbursements.

Follow these steps as closely as possible when handling rent payments:

- Make a copy of any form of payment you receive except cash, such as checks or money orders. If you get cash, you can provide a written receipt and make a copy.

How to Handle the Money

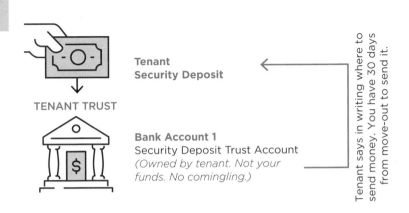

1

Tenant Security Deposit

TENANT TRUST

Bank Account 1
Security Deposit Trust Account
(Owned by tenant. Not your funds. No comingling.)

Tenant says in writing where to send money. You have 30 days from move-out to send it.

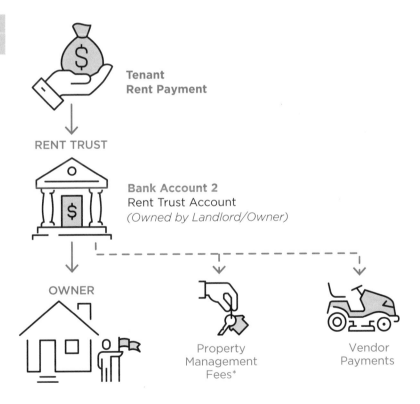

2

Tenant Rent Payment

RENT TRUST

Bank Account 2
Rent Trust Account
(Owned by Landlord/Owner)

OWNER

Property Management Fees*

Vendor Payments

*If you're self-managing the property, the money goes straight to you, the property owner.

- Make a copy of your deposit slip that corresponds with the cash/checks you receive and attach them together. If you receive direct deposit, print the record and attach it to your bank statement when reconciling.
- Take the extra steps to move the money to the appropriate account(s) even if you have to move it two times—into an operating account for example. You want to honor the protocol of who owns what and the necessary steps to protect it.
- If you pay your vendors electronically, print records to use in reconciliation and attach printouts to invoices or work orders.
- Keep the records for seven years.
- Again, if you handle cash, don't pay yourself from it. Put it in accounts first.
- Keep things locked up. Account numbers and financial records are important to protect.
- Be organized by documenting dates, making copies, and having things buttoned up. Provide a receipt if the tenant asks, especially if your only option is cash.

Paying Vendors or Yourself

Once rent money is submitted, it must clear the bank. If you are a property manager or if you have multiple properties, wait for funds to clear the bank prior to any disbursements. Otherwise, your accounting may become complicated, particularly if any discrepancies or deficiencies arise. And if you pay yourself for a repair, talk to a CPA first. You may need estimates to justify and document the expense.

Our rents are due on the first day of the month and considered late after the fifth day. Then we wait until the fifteenth to do disbursements, giving payments at least ten days to clear, so all the issues related to the funds have ample chance to get worked out.

If the rent is late, don't disperse the funds until the rent payment has cleared the bank. This generally takes about ten days unless funds are wired or certified. Pay the owner and vendors first and the fees to yourself second.

Returning the Security Deposit

When a tenant moves out, the keys are returned, and you have done a walk-through inspection with all of their stuff out of the house, then tenant begins the quest to get their deposit back. This is when all the hidden bumps and bruises will appear, and the dance begins to mitigate any repairs. Here is the process:

- Perform the inspection only when the tenant is completely out. (That means keys are returned.)
- Get quotes for any repairs and save them for reconciliation.
- Send an accounting of the repairs in written form along with a check for the remainder of the security deposit.
- Do all of the above *before* 5:00 p.m. on the thirtieth day after the tenant moves out. If you need more time, send a letter explaining why and how long you will need to gather estimates or the disposition of all the funds from the deposits. Several states have this thirty-day requirement, and if you miss it, you may have to refund the entire security deposit regardless of necessary repairs. Ask your attorney or real estate broker about the rules in your state.

When returning all or a portion of the security deposit to the tenant, it is best to move the money from the tenant security deposit trust account into a checking account, and then pay the tenant. We operate here under the direction of the owner if we are the property manager. If you own the property and make a deduction, you will need to document clearly what you have done. You are expected to allow for normal wear and tear.

The theme for accounting for the money is to document everything and have a trail of the money from the moment it leaves the tenant and every moment and every month it is in your possession.

If you are making a claim for damages, send the costs and damage request in writing. File in a small claims court if you wish to seek damages or hire a collection agency to take on the calls. But make sure you have the right documentation. Right or wrong, the documentation determines whether you win or lose in almost every case. Without it, you don't stand a chance.

Reconciliation

Each of your accounts and each tenant's accounts should be reconciled monthly. In the real world, if every tenant paid on time and if every owner got paid on time, then the rental bank account every month would be zero. What comes in goes completely out. But sometimes tenants are late, or they pay a partial month, or whatever.

Reconcile the individual accounts first and the total of all accounts second. Make sure that no fees (such as maintenance costs, HOA dues, or taxes) are paid from the tenant's security deposit trust account. Otherwise, you are taking the tenant's money to pay those fees, and that is not legal. Pay fees from a separate operating account. Each month, when reconciling the trust accounts, you must also check the money going in, money going out, and disposition of what is in the owner's account and why, for example, a maintenance reserve or to cover an HOA fee or taxes.

For record keeping, I won't tell folks how or what to use (yes, many still do it manually); however, I do recommend getting some accounting software that can do some of the record-keeping work for you. If you don't like to do accounting or bookkeeping, get a bookkeeper to help you. Make sure they understand how things should be accounted for and the need for reconciliations and rules around fees.

If you established an LLC for your investment property and are taking rent payments, make sure payments are made to the LLC, not to yourself individually. And make sure you provide yourself a 1099 for the income or whatever other forms your accountant says you need. Keep the money and the liability at arm's length to make sure you can garner all the benefits. How you pay yourself and how you account for your expenses will keep you straight for tax purposes. Set up a system with your CPA.

Transfers from One House to Another

Property managers and people who own multiple properties may sometimes borrow from one house's income to pay for another house's issues. In such cases, itemization and documentation are even more important. If you're a property manager, make sure you only make transfers under the same ownership and that each home's in-and-out is documented clearly and that the renter has proper credit for rent paid in the tenant ledger/account you are moving the rental proceeds from.

Who Is Watching

If you are managing trust accounts and are a licensed real estate agent, I guarantee you that the real estate commission is watching. We get a newsletter every month, and in the very back are the disciplinary actions by agent and area. Well over half of the folks in trouble mishandled money in trust accounts. Don't let that happen to you.

Let me tell you who else is watching: the tenant. Many tenants know the laws even better than most agents or property managers do. Don't think for one minute they don't know that you have their money and the rules and laws that surround it. One of my staff missed the thirty-day notification window once and had to refund a whole security deposit. I will never make that mistake again.

Interest and Fees on Trust Accounts

You must have permission in writing from the owner of the account (i.e., either the tenant or the property owner) to collect interest on trust accounts. Although in my opinion, the accounting that goes along with that tiny amount of money is not worth it. Again, these are the laws in the state of North Carolina. Don't assume they are the same for your state.

Watch out for those bank fees. Many states have rules about fees on trust accounts. You can deposit just enough to counter fees, but be aware of how much you deposit as that could be a problem for you.

Account for the Money
Key Takeaways

Document everything when it comes to money to avoid accounting and potentially legal headaches.

Do not intermingle the tenant's money with yours.

Make note of your state's rules regarding money held in trust, particularly the required documentation and any relevant time limits.

Do not use security deposit as rent. NO! NO! NO!

Notes

_____

_____

_____

_____

_____

Caring for the home

is a critical part of the lease.

CHAPTER 10

Perform Inspections

Recently, we scheduled an inspection in a home. A renter was really good and compliant as it relates to the move-in, money, and documents. As I drove up to the house, the exterior was well manicured and clean, and the yard was picked up and tidy. Ever since they moved in a couple months prior to inspection, they paid rent on time. No problems.

Wrong. I walked into the house. They had one dog listed on the lease—and it had a new friend. Also, the husband who had recently retired kept a very clean house, kept nice candles burning, and I immediately knew why. He was a smoker. And he was smoking inside.

I stated immediately that not only was the new dog an issue, but also the smoking was absolutely a violation of the lease. He clearly stated he did not know. Immediately, I told him that claim was ridiculous as he signed an addendum on smoking, and I was coming back to check on him. If he continued to smoke in the home, he would be evicted. Further, he was responsible for remediating the smoke and all the costs associated with it. As nice as they are, and good as they pay, they too cannot stay. I also told his wife, who traveled frequently, of his inside habit, and I believe that put the fear of God in him as well.

Before we get into the subject of inspections, make sure you have the rights to enter your property with proper notice or in the event of an emergency. You must have that very clearly spelled out in your lease. Also make sure you have an extra set of keys. In case they do change the locks, make sure the lease says that after proper notification of inspection, you have the right to enter and charge them for any costs associated with rekeying the property. Also remember that you are there to check the condition of the house, not judge their housekeeping. This is a fine line of care though. If the home is really filthy, note it, photo it, and schedule another inspection for seven days later as there are limits to what is acceptable.

Also make sure your inspection includes external buildings to verify they are not sublet or having issues. One time, we were working with a new owner to take over a house and provide a list of make-ready changes to get the house ready to go. How the previous manager missed what was in the external garage is beyond me. Our property manager met the new owner at the site to review the list. He walked out to the external garage only to find a hot tub, multiple mirrors, and a stripper pole installed in the center of the garage that was "NOT STRUCTURAL" in nature. So I guess there was no question that they were very much OK with parking the car outside. Oh man, that is just not something you can unsee.

Remember: just because they pay their rent on time does not mean they have a right to stay. Caring for the home is a critical part of the lease. Paying their rent is important, of course, but it is just one part of having a successful tenancy.

Setting up Inspections

After you got your home rent-ready in chapter 4, you documented the condition of the interior and exterior before any tenants moved in. That initial documentation is your benchmark. Now, you will hold regular inspections to document the life of the property (how it changes with tenants and time), to handle any necessary repairs in a timely manner, and to identify and document damage and any potential policy violations on the part of your tenants.

Remember that the tenant should have received the move-in inspection form we spoke of in chapter 8, so they could note any issues they saw when they moved in, and you could sign off on those same conditions. When they return their form, see if there is anything you need to handle, and then document when and how you handle that as well. Notice a theme? **Hint:** *documentation.* If it isn't properly documented, it never really happened. It always amazes me how a tenant's memory can be sharp on some things and dull on others. You get my drift here.

I love to do the first inspection at the property five days after the person moves in. They have spent a few nights in there, so you can see any move-in damage and evidence of any surprise occupants (people or pets) that were not disclosed up front.

I once got an enraged call from a tenant at inspection time. He was a stay-at-home dad while the wife worked. He said they were very private people and that I had no right to do an inspection, that I was intrusive and not entitled to do so. Later, enraged, they refused to let us come in and check on the status of our client's property. Well, according to our lease, we give twenty-four-hour notice by email, phone, or text, and whether they answer or not, we are coming in—and we did. The house was fine, but they continued to be enraged. After another face-to-face meeting where we were verbally abused for simply protecting our client's property, we asked them to move out and gave them proper notice. They did. They acted like homeowners, which is great in one sense, but they forgot one important fact: they did not own the home.

Your lease should require you to give tenants advance notice before entering, but you can do surprise drive-by inspections of the exterior, and that can tell you a lot and present some warning signs, like seeing cars parked in the yard.

How Often

How often you perform inspections is subjective. I prefer two to three times a year, more if justified. In some cases, I do them once a month because of issues inherent with the properties (keeping an eye on some water drainage, for example) or the tenants. Don't be a pest but do explain the property is an asset you must protect; the inspection is nothing personal. Do them on a regular schedule and consistently follow the step-by-step instructions below.

Inspections Step by Step

Follow this process without any shortcuts. Shortcuts send a message that the inspection isn't all that important. But it is serious business since they are in a very expensive asset.

1. Give tenants notice and an opportunity to respond at least twenty-four hours before your inspection. If they want to be there but have time constraints, try to work with them as you can as long as they're cooperative. Cooperative means answering the correspondence and an attitude of reasonable cooperation to make it happen.

2. Before going in, check the lease to remember who should be living there, whether or not pets are approved, and if so, how many and what type.

3. Review previous inspection reports and take copies with you, so you know what to look for and can compare any damage or issues against your existing benchmark. Also see if any stains in ceilings and things on the existing reports have gotten any worse, which could mean your inspection is a preventative measure, not just a timely check in.

4. Take photos of each side of the exterior and make note of any areas that need attention. In addition to giving you an ongoing record of conditions, they may also be helpful if an insurance claim is ever needed.

Things to look for on the outside:

    a. Make sure trees are not rubbing against the house, roof, or overhangs, which could cause damage.

    b. Look for wood rot on the exterior or overfilled gutters or low spots where moisture or other water exists.

    c. Check the yard for grass conditions or other things that stand out about general care.

    d. Look on the roof for satellite dishes that are not approved. (Satellite dish companies require the homeowners' permission before installing a dish.)

    e. Finally, look for any HOA violations like trash cans out too long or left in sight of the road, cars parked on the street where not allowed, or other things that would be a red flag when the nosy neighbors or HOA police come by.

5. When you step inside, ask the tenant, "Can you share with me any issues you are having?" This will tell you right away things you may not be able to easily detect. Then photograph each room.

Things to look for inside:

    a. Make sure no locks have been added to interior doors that were not formerly there. It could be a sign of a possible challenge. (More on that later.)

    b. Check the filters. This is the lung of the HVAC system. If it is clogged, the system cannot breathe, and the possibility for mildew or mold problems increase. Sweating vents may be a sign of dirty filters and poor airflow.

    c. Check all appliances to make sure they're in good working condition.

    d. Test the smoke and carbon monoxide detectors. Your lease should note that tenants are responsible for replacing batteries in both detectors and the thermostat at least once a year. Note in your inspection report if they have not been changed, so you can follow up in writing.

e. Check floors, ceilings, and walls for any damage. It may be harder to really see behind curtains and furniture, but again if you have questions to ask the tenant, ask them.

f. Look at wall colors. Are they the same as when the tenant moved in? Or did someone paint a room with chalk paint or black paint? This is a clear lease violation and needs to be addressed while they are there, not when they move out, if possible. Unless they get permission in writing, no painting should have occurred.

g. Look for safety issues. A grill in the garage is a big one. If they grill in the garage, it's a huge red flag. Other safety issues we see are the storage of items close to the water heater or heat source and extra-dirty stoves and ovens. The tenant is expected to keep the unit up, not use it up.

6. You must have access to every room. They know you're coming, so wake any sleepers.

7. After the inspection, send the tenant a copy of the photos, including notification of any actions required on their part and by when. If you're a property manager, send a copy to the owner. Note whether any issues discovered during the inspection merit a reinspection and when.

8. When everything is handled properly, send the tenant a follow-up thank-you note or email.

Tenant Repairs for Inspection Violations

Sometimes inspections uncover issues the tenant is responsible for addressing. We'll talk more about repairs in the next chapter, but I want to share my hard-and-fast rules and clear boundaries regarding tenant repairs:

1. Use licensed technicians in the appropriate fields for all repairs. For example, a licensed electrician should fix electrical issues but not plumbing issues.

2. To get repairs done the right way, not necessarily the cheapest way, avoid owner and tenant repairs whenever possible.

3. If tenants insist on doing the repairs because they believe they can save money doing it themselves, just be sure to reinspect. You do have the right to say no—it's not their house.

4. If you hire technicians on behalf of the tenant, *do not* mark up invoices. Be fair and have receipts.

5. Be in control of who fixes what. Hire your own vendors.

Incentive Program

Many property management companies and owners offer incentives to tenants around inspections. Here is a program I developed called the Gold Star Tenant Program. It offers gift cards based on a point system. You can decide if they have multiple times a year to get incentives. You can offer points when the conditions below are met upon inspection:

- Filters changed (3 points)
- House clean and well kept (3 points)
- Yard neat and clean (3 points)
- On time for inspection appointment (3 points)
- Rent paid on time (5 points)
- Batteries in smoke and CO detectors and thermostats working when tested (5 points)
- Renters insurance paid annually (5 points)

The Incognito Owner

Wanting to own investment property does not necessarily mean you want tenants to have direct access to you. But some of our owner clients are very handy and want to handle maintenance and inspections themselves. We absolutely have no problem with this, and it's really a great way to save money if you have the skills. We help them stay incognito by giving them hats with our company logo and using their middle names with the tenant. The tenant has no idea the owner is the handyman.

It's funny how things can happen. One of my owners was working in his house and painting incognito. The tenants approached him asking if he thought the owner would approve replacing the oven. He said to call the property manager and ask as he did not know. So they did right there and then. About two minutes later, my team called him, and his cell phone rang with us on the line. He hit that handy little "ignore" button on the side of his phone. He called me afterwards, and we had a good laugh over the chain of events. To this day, they don't know it's him. He gets to work on his property without the hassle of tenant manipulation.

Triggers for Additional Inspections

We were managing a three-bedroom townhome close to the rail line that led to uptown Charlotte. The tenant screening was clean, and the first month's rent came in on time. No issues. At our month two inspection, every bedroom had an additional lock on the door. Occupancy on the lease said two people, yet each room looked like a different person was living there. One room even had a small fridge. Well, I am guessing you've already figured out what we quickly knew—he was subletting rooms for a combined amount well over his lease and pocketing the excess balance. As we found out later, he did not even live there.

In today's world with Airbnb and other room subletting sites, you have to be careful to look for signs of things that don't match the lease or intended use, even in suburbia or large country club communities. Your lease should have a clear statement regarding sublease, and it's a great reason to do an inspection.

Here are some triggers for additional inspections beyond your normal schedule:

- Late rent
- Discord among roommates
- Odd maintenance requests
- Recurring maintenance requests, such as clogged drains
- HOA complaints
- Poor housekeeping at previous inspections
- Poor exterior condition upon drive-by inspection
- Lack of communication and follow up
- Inconsistent interior changes
- Independent living conditions inside the house, such as a fridge or hot plate in the bedrooms and/or the presence of suitcases in the rooms

Perform Inspections
Key Takeaways

Protect your investment with regular inspections to monitor the condition of your property and mitigate any problems.

Document everything. Always.

Offer incentives for good behavior.

Notes

It's one thing to be **accommodating** and another to be **run over**.

CHAPTER 11

Manage Repairs

Let me tell a story about a tenant named Jed,
a tenant who moved in to keep his family ahead,
and then one day he was putting up his food,
and inside the fridge was a bulb no longer good.

Burnt out it was, black as night, not shining bright.

Well the first thing you know ol' Jed is on the phone,
calling every number to get someone to hear his moan,
and once he does, he starts shooting up their ears
cause he can't see the label on his beers.

Git here now, he says, it's an emergency.

Hopefully, you sang that in your head to the tune of the *Beverly Hillbillies* theme song. Houses need repairs—that's never been an argument any of us need to spend time discussing—but the topic can be open-ended and volatile, both from the owner side and the tenant side. This subject was actually the impetus for opening my own property management company. How do you handle repairs? What makes sense? How do you structure it? How do you balance it? I think

I could probably write a whole book about repairs, but I will just work on completing this one.

Understand that repairs are going to be necessary. Some fall upon the owner, and some fall upon the tenant. It takes bravery to call out a tenant in their negligence, and although it's rare, sometimes tenants (usually former homeowners) will take responsibility for the mishap. These tenants are a true gift. They also understand that houses require maintenance, and sometimes necessary repairs cause inconvenience, and it is not intentional or the fault of the homeowner or management company when stuff breaks.

Valid versus Nonvalid Repairs

Let's start with valid versus nonvalid repairs. Valid repairs are those you would fix whether someone lived there or not. Just like humans, houses break down with age. It just happens. Sometimes gremlins get into the water heater or HVAC unit and cause chaos, but for the most part, wear and tear is an expected phenomenon in any house. The real lesson here is one I drive home throughout this whole book: document and communicate even if they don't want to hear what you have to say. If it's a valid repair, continue working through it, and if the tenant makes things difficult for access, document that too.

Invalid repairs include things like drywall tape showing, burned out light bulbs, ants in the cabinet because they left food open, the neighbor's grass is not cut, the water pressure is not enough to make our guests happy, the pool in the HOA won't let us swim naked (just kidding, kind of), the blinds on the house are not opaque enough—you get the picture. "Nonvalid" doesn't mean nothing needs fixing nor does it imply fault by the tenant. Most tenants could take care of these issues themselves, but if they can't or simply won't, you can still perform the repair—just make sure the tenant pays for the service call and materials, not you (or the owner if you're the property manager).

Sometimes you can cause more harm by not going ahead and paying for something. Use your discretion. Sometimes the little things can set the tone. Just remember that what you do or don't do is still a balancing act, so it's one thing to be accommodating and another to be run over. If you do cover tenant repairs, document it and let the tenant know that if it happens again, they will pay.

Special note for property managers: many times when you don't respond the way a tenant wants or as fast as they want, or you call out their negligence, they will go to the tax records, seek out the owner's name and mailing address, and reach out to them about how you have not responded to them, how you are rude and don't return their calls, and so forth. Here is how to fix it: document everything, every conversation, and let the owner know when you run into a situation that could prove to discredit you. This is a clear reason to have a strong software management system that integrates and structures and documents everything. If the owner finds out from the tenant before you tell them, you have already lost. A great conversation to have with a new owner when they come on board with you: tell them that by contract you work for the them, not the tenants, and that tenants will do whatever they can to get what they want when they want it. Also tell them that if you tell the tenant no, it is really a no and in the owner's best interest—they need to trust you. Also tell Mr. or Mrs. Owner that they don't need to respond to those calls or emails; simply forward them to you.

Special note for owners: if you don't use a management company, many of the same things apply when it comes to nonvalid repairs. Case in point: a bulb was burned out on the front porch at one of my rentals in Cincinnati. The tenant wanted to know when I was going to change it. They said they felt unsafe, so it was an emergency, and the light was in the common area, which was not their responsibility. My response—the one I gave, not the little thought bubble that we all get when we want to tell someone to take a flying leap—was that since I lived in Charlotte, North Carolina, I would not be there any time soon to change the light bulb. Instead, I would reimburse them for the cost of a full package of bulbs and send them a gift card for their trouble and asked if they would just go ahead and change it for me.

Their Repairs versus Yours

About 70 percent of the time, tenants call with legitimate repair requests. Some requests can be addressed immediately, and some may only be an emergency to them but in reality just a slight inconvenience till a vendor can schedule a fix. But to that point, if you have documentation for a repair, and it is their fault, they should expect to be charged and should be charged. If they do not have the money to cover their transgressions, consider financing the repair if it is significant. For example, a tenant's son hit the garage door with the car. They did not have all the funds to fix it, so with the owner's permission, we allowed them to pay for the repair in two installments. Will tenants argue over repairs they are charged for? Yup, it's probable. Just charge them anyway and run your property like a business.

Receiving Requests

Valid or nonvalid, set clear parameters on how you accept and deal with repairs. I recommend you receive all repairs via email or, if you have one, within your automated property management software. Real emergencies can have a different process, which we'll talk about later. Let tenants know that if they do not get a response within twenty-four hours, they can text you with the same request.

Why not take repair requests by phone? Because it's harder to document than a timed and dated email. Imagine arguing with a tenant who says they called and left a voicemail, when truly the tenant never called to begin with. I am absolutely over that ridiculous argument. Our move-in instructions clearly state to use our portal system to document any repair requests. It's clear, concise, and makes the argument a nonstarter.

I once got an angry email from a tenant's dad, who claimed his daughter had been without water for three weeks. She was doing laundry at a laundromat and showering elsewhere. He claimed we owed his daughter back rent. Well, we called the tenant. She admitted that she never called us, never sent in the issue, and we were not made aware of the urgency of the matter. Of course, her father said we should have known anyway. Well, indeed it would be nice to be all knowing, ever seeing, and have the gift of prophecy—I'd own Wall Street. Until then, email all your service requests. By the way, she was without water because she did not pay her water bill, and the city shut off the water.

Scheduling

Sometimes scheduling repairs feels like forcing the moon, stars, and planets to align. You have two agendas (the tenant's and the vendor's) that are opposing forces but have the same goal. When it works, you hear an angel chorus as the clouds open up and warm sunshine falls on your face as you look up and smile.

For vendor visits, many tenants want to be home when the vendor comes for the simple reason that they feel more comfortable. Others really don't care—they just want it done. The problem comes when the tenant wants the vendor to come in a tight window or on weekends. That won't always work out—no more moon and stars, just dark skies and thunder. I will say, however, that if the tenant has been a homeowner in the past, it helps. They understand that many vendors do not work evenings and weekends. That is another great instance where having a tenant that was previously a homeowner helps. Interesting aside: 34 percent of the senior population (former homeowners) now rents. This is the main reason I like ranches. I want to be able to provide an option for this generation because it's growing rapidly.

Make sure you have contractual clarity about access. Your lease should very clearly state that with proper notice, usually twenty-four hours, you can access the property whether they want you to or not, or in the case of an emergency, you can go in immediately. Many owners get into hot water here by accessing the property without documented access requests. They don't understand that tenants have rights, and owners get themselves into hot water by accessing the property without following proper protocol—I mean seriously hot water. Just because you own it doesn't mean you can go in whenever you want. If you are a tenant reading this, and you shoot your landlord for accessing the home without authority, don't shoot them in the yard; if you do, drag them back inside. (P.S. Really just don't shoot your landlord.)

Remember the communication matrix in chapter 2? If not, go back and review since it definitely comes into play here. Here's how the process works in a repair scheduling situation:

1. The tenant documents an issue by email or through your online portal.
2. You or the appropriate member of your team contacts the vendor and provides documentation of the situation, the property address, the tenant's contact information, and instructions to connect directly with the tenant.
3. Document your contact with the vendor.
4. Contact the tenant to share the vendor's contact information in case they don't hear from the vendor in a timely manner. Document that too.
5. Steps 2 through 4 repeat to confirm that an appointment is

scheduled and that work has been completed, all the while keeping the property owner informed (also documented).

Handling Charges

If you are an owner who handles repairs yourself (incognito or otherwise), remember than you cannot charge yourself or the tenant for your labor in most cases, just for materials. It becomes really dicey if you charge for anything other than materials if it ends up before a magistrate. If you want to document your materials and time for tax purposes, talk to your CPA.

If you work with a property management company, set very clear protocols on how charges will be handled. Our contract states that owners allow us to take care of any repairs without authorization up to $250 or $500 (the owner chooses). Above that we get approval. We hold a $250 reserve for the owner for small incidentals, and if we use any of that balance, we replace it at the next rent cycle.

Sometimes tenants will ask to take the repair charge out of their security deposit. That's a nonstarter—say no and save that money for the end of the lease. That coffer will never get refilled, and they will use it like a Christmas fund. You need that money as leverage to counterbalance their exit transgressions.

It is very rare to get a tenant to pay for any self-inflicted damage or mistakes without stress and arguments. Where we see the largest amount of resistance is when the tenant fails to show up for the vendor appointment, but the vendor still charges for the trip. This always cracks me up because you will hear all about how they didn't get confirmation. Again, documentation is what will save the day here. Texts back and forth can further strengthen your position. We have a system that will send, receive, and document texts. As a matter of process, you can send them an invoice and make it payable with their next rent payment. Again, just make sure you clearly document the reason for the charge.

If you decide to forgive the charge, make sure you document to the tenant what you've done, and if it happens again and if they do not pay the next time, then both charges will then become due. Harsh? No, just realistic. Remember that this is a judgment call. It's just like eating tiny portions on big plates of froufrou food when your spouse wants to try the new restaurant; sometimes you give a little to keep harmony. When lease renewal comes around, weigh out the validity of keeping the tenant and don't be afraid to make a change.

Choosing Vendors

If you have a home warranty, make sure you use it. The warranty may dictate the particular vendor. If you work with a warranty company on your properties, note that if they don't have someone available right away, call back and make them give you another provider, especially when it comes to the bigger issues like HVAC, electrical, and plumbing.

Management companies have a leg up here as most have a pool of vendors they use regularly. A good relationship and consistent work lead to competitive pricing and quick response. You can always find cheaper services, but response time trumps price in all cases.

If you're a property manager, note that some owners have their own vendors. Use them, and again document and keep them in your systems.

Owners, don't let your vendors cause discord with tenants—make sure you have backups in case of scheduling problems. And if you use a management company and they are using your vendors, run it all through the management company, which gives you complete and consolidated accounting.

Let's discuss my theory on the trades for a minute: when the economy is good, and a handyman or tradesman says they're not busy at all, you better think twice. That can mean either they just moved here or you should run away and run fast. For sure, you want someone you can trust and who is available. But you also don't want someone just coming off a nice jaunt where they blew off all their business at the last minute to go to a fishing tournament sponsored by Jack Daniels with their brother-in-law.

My rule: the trades you use should not be on your payroll, and management companies should not have their hands in any of the repair charges. Last year, on behalf our clients, we managed over $250,000 of repairs and maintenance requests. Sure, 20 percent of that would be a nice chunk. But that is not the role of a property manager. If you are charged with managing a property, that is where you make your money, and that business practice draws a clear line on where your interests lie. My only exception is when I have to send one of my staff members out to the property to be on-site to supervise a complicated or expensive repair. In such cases, I will charge the owner 7 percent of the repair cost. I have placed that charge fewer than ten times, and the owner knew about it well in advance.

I'll Just Call My Guy

The secret to the property management and property investment business, whether long-term rentals, short-term rentals, or vacation rentals, is to "have a guy." That is not a gender reference; it is a true and necessary property term that leads to your bottom-line success. If you have a plumbing problem, you have a guy for that.

Even more important is to have the kind of guy who can fix or patch just about anything. Extreme case in point: I got a call from a rental property's neighbor. A deer had gotten hit by a car about a quarter mile away and had given us the distinct honor of wandering into our back yard to lay down and die. It really was amazing that it chose us within such a dense subdivision … or maybe the neighbor dragged it there. Anyway, when I got the call to handle it, the deer was no longer nimble if you get my drift. Now what?

Call animal control? No. County waste management? No. Critter Gitter? Yes! Oh, wait … $500? Heck no. So I called "my guy," my Mr. Can-Do-Anything guy. He dragged the deer onto a landscape trailer and took him to the appropriate "disposal area" for 150 "bucks." (See what I did there?)

You gotta have a guy who can be there and will come whenever you need them, within reason, and is able to handwrite an invoice. I recommend getting two of every trade: two general handymen, two electricians, two HVAC specialists, and two plumbers. National chains and citywide services are great, but community-minded tradesman are always the best. I love husband-and-wife teams in the trades: the wife does the bookwork and scheduling and, just like a marriage, is always telling her husband what to do and where to go.

When it comes to vacation property or short-term rentals, you are surely all about your online ratings. That makes it even more important to have a good, local hands-on person. That will truly make or break your income experience. As you might guess, cleaning people are the first anchor in any vacation rental. Everyone has their own level of "clean," so if your cleaning people are not hands-on with great attention to detail, you are sunk before you start. At the very least, make sure they are willing to put out soft toilet tissue, soap, and garbage bags. Buy it yourself at a large warehouse store if you have to and give it to them. And send "your guy" a gift at Christmas. They love that stuff and know how much you appreciate them.

Get your partnerships in order quickly. You won't have a chance to meet them all, but try to meet the majority. Here are a few places to find them:

- Referral from your property management company.
- Better Business Bureau.
- A property investor club.
- Neighbor.
- Local chamber of commerce—these are among my favorites because these are people invested in community.

- Referral from other property investors
- Realtors®—if you work with a Realtor® who understands investment, they will likely have these folks on standby.
- Construction sites—talk to folks on a jobsite. Many of the crews do jobs on the side.
- Golf courses—landscapers are hard to find. Many a great landscaper will come to your house when they are done with their shifts.
- Fireman—they are great at so many things.
- Community websites where you can get references from neighbors.
- HOA manager.

What Qualifies as a Real Emergency?

Many years ago, as I began working with tenants as the owner of my first investment property, I learned a very valuable lesson. What may be an emergency to some may not be an emergency to others. The size of the emergency doesn't matter; it's the emotion that escalates around an issue that can take a very commonplace issue and make it a real or imagined emergency in an instant.

For example, a light being out is not really an emergency. But it can feel like one when the tenant dropped her keys in the dark and scrambled to find them and could not because the front porch light just burned out. I got a real chewin' over that, and she wanted immediate results from her call. Or if little Junior just dropped his favorite car into the A/C vent and has not stopped crying for ten hours, that can feel like an emergency. And now my most favorite of all time—yes, this happened. In Cincinnati, there are many old neighborhoods. Houses there are part of an underground, interconnected sewer system that has been there for years. The city maintains those underground systems through a series of tunnels and manholes. And as you can guess, critters live down there, more specifically the four-legged furry kind with long tails. Well, it just so happened that one of the rats from the sewer system made its way up the iron pipe channel into our main floor bathroom. By opening the flapper, it can make its way into the bowl (now you know why toilet lids were actually invented) while someone I know, aka my wife, just so happened to be using the toilet. Yes, now that's an emergency—a pants-around-your-ankles, screaming, running-through-the-house emergency. Ben (from the movie *Ben*) invaded our home and was going to bite her on the you-know-what. When we called the city, they shared stories of people shooting their toilets with guns thinking it would solve the problem. How about no?

I think you get the point. Sometimes real emergencies happen, and even true life-and-death emergencies happen in homes. It's a serious matter but also one that needs to be tempered with reality. As a property manager and owner, know the whole story, make clear decisions, and pick up the phone and listen. It can diffuse many of the concerns that escalate in these hairy situations. I can easily lay out some very clear parameters for what denotes an emergency and what does not. But if your tenant has renter's insurance and if necessary in a true emergency of fire or flood, their policy will pick up coverage for a place to stay and a backup plan to cover any possessions of the owner or tenant.

True Emergencies

- Fire is the biggie. I am not talking about a small grease fire here but a true fire that causes smoke damage or damage to the property to make the home uninhabitable.
- Water can truly make things go downhill quickly. I am not talking about localized water or even a wet area or two. I mean water that reaches a certain height or flowing in a way that causes real harm to possessions, structure or property. We once got a call that a water heater was leaking, and the floors were getting damaged. It is an emergency *if* cool heads

don't prevail to turn off the water and the breaker on the electrical water heater. But not having hot water does not constitute an emergency, just an uncomfortable shower.

- If you have only one bathroom and it is inoperable, in the eyes of the court, that means immediate action is eminent. You must provide at least one working bathroom.
- The absence of heat on days cooler than freezing is considered an emergency. You can make alternative plans for this by stocking backup electric heaters. It's much easier to fix that issue when you can provide heat alternatively and get it fixed on a non-overtime basis.
- Lack of water in the house is an emergency. While you are not required to pay their utility bill, the house must have access to clean, running water.
- Damage to the roof that allows water in, especially during a storm, is a true emergency.
- A sewer backup into the house, yes, absolutely makes the list. A couple of years ago, the town near us would routinely blow out the sewer lines. Well, it did exactly that—blew out my neighbor's toilet, and the sewage formed a volcano in their hall bath. This also includes septic backup, which can happen. However, it does not include when tenants clog the drain with hair or grease or toys.
- A break-in is an emergency that requires immediate attention on all fronts. Protect them and the property without hesitation.
- Microbial growth (MOLD) should be fixed IMMEDIATELY.
- A zombie apocalypse would qualify, but if they have zombie insurance, it really helps.

Emergency Look-Alikes
- No air conditioning is bad of course, especially if you have little kids, but again back-up window units or spare fans help here. Get it fixed as quick as possible, but it's not a true emergency.

- Broken appliances, no matter how much you love to cook, are not true emergencies.
- Power outages are a pain but aren't usually in the control of the homeowner. It's an inconvenience and could result in food loss, but rental policies can allow for help there. Unless the outage is a direct result of a known issue, do your best to help the tenant and use common sense. I do treat it like a very high-priority issue with my rentals if it is something I can control, especially when children and the elderly are involved.
- Broken windows should be secured and fixed, but you aren't required to find a glass blower ASAP.
- Neighbor noise is not in your control. Tell them to call the police.
- Washers and dryers becoming inoperable is not an emergency. This is why I don't include them in my properties, nor should you. Laundromats are available for use, and many are open for twenty-four hours.
- Beeping smoke detectors—yup, you get it.
- Downed fences or trees are not emergencies unless they impede access or have damaged the home. If power lines are down, they should call the power company for help and, of course, let you know.
- Bugs, snakes, and intrusive noises are not an emergency but should be investigated.

These are a few examples of many. You must really help the tenant understand that some things have to wait. Hearing them out and providing them calm, clear instructions on how and when the issue will be handled makes a difference. Don't ignore them; just be clear and concise and, by all means, put it in writing and complete the loop to make sure all the follow-up happens.

Keeping the Tenant Happy

A happy tenant is icing on the cake for a good return on your investment. It reminds me of the broken-window principle. In New York City, they did a study of areas with high crime and vandalism, most of which had a lot of empty, dilapidated buildings. Then they went in and fixed all the broken windows and cleaned up the buildings. As a result, crime went down substantially. Well, the same goes for your rental home. If you care for it, there is a stronger likelihood that they will too. Sometimes it seems like a test. The demands of a tenant seem to intensify early in the lease, and if you listen and handle things that are appropriate, you tend to get more grace in the long term. Of course, this varies by tenant and home, but it's the underlying principle of it that matters.

Sometimes minor issues offer opportunities to create good will with a tenant. Send them a written note—it's documentation again—that while you know the issue is their responsibility, you want to invest in a good start or a continued positive relationship. It's cheaper than vacancy. If the same thing happens again, you know your good will is not appreciated and can move forward with charging them for their actions. I do this sometimes with late fees or small incidental issues. It keeps the windows from being broken on the way out. Like most things, if handled the right way, the result can be rewarding.

Manage Repairs
Key Takeaways

Use the communication matrix on page 40 and document every step of the way: when the repair was requested, what was requested, what you're doing about it, when it was resolved, who resolved it, and when you closed the loop with the tenant and owner.

If you have to pay for a few tenant-inflicted blunders to keep the peace, do so but put tight parameters on repeat offenders.

Keep a deep bench of qualified vendors.

Document everything. Make sure requests come in via email or in a form that you can time/date stamp and track.

Notes

Damage lurks

where furniture
and pictures
hang out.

CHAPTER 12

Move Them Out

If you want the simple version of this chapter, go to chapter 9 and read it backwards. Everyone thinks that this is an easy process—once they are ready to go and get their stuff out, it's a done deal. We *always* get requests for the move-out inspection to be done a week or so before they move, and they *always* want their security deposit back the moment they turn in the keys. Not gonna happen. Since so many tenants share this expectation, I'll explain why we don't do it this way.

The simple answer is that damage lurks where furniture and pictures hang out. Even the best tenants may have issues under their stuff that they're unaware of. But the majority know about it and want to either hide it or say the damage was there before they moved in. This is why the move-in inspection and ongoing inspections are so important. It's not that you want to keep their money, and normal wear and tear is considered—it's because things happen.

I remember one tenant who thought we were the belle of the ball. We were so good to her, and she loved our communication so much that she was going to recommend us to all her friends. During her tenancy, we had even painted the whole house to make her happy. We were nothing short of awesome—until her move-out inspection.

Well, she had hung pictures all over the house—tons of them—and instead of following the terms of the lease, she patched every hole with a smear of plaster. Every wall in every room was covered in white smears. If you read our lease, it specifies not to make nail holes. We charged her for a paint job. Guess what—we became the evil spawn. You can make someone sign the lease, but that's no guarantee they actually read it.

Move-Out Rules

1. Make sure your lease and even your move-in instructions specify when and how the security deposit will be returned. As mentioned in chapter 9, North Carolina has a thirty-day time limit unless you specify in writing a reason for delay. Find out your state's laws about the disposition of security deposits and how charges against it are handled, but remember that if you perform the repairs yourself and overcharge, you may not be worth per hour what a judge says you are. Save the receipts and get quotes from others to give yourself a chance.

2. Get the keys back. Move out is not complete without the keys. The property is considered still in their possession until the keys hit your hand. Just because they are in the mail, it does not constitute a release. The final inspection only happens with the keys in your possession.

3. Get the utilities out of their name as soon as you get the keys back. Take possession of the expenses. If they have a balance, it's on them. Never agree to pay any utilities for them or from their deposit.

4. Provide a list for the tenant of items they must take care of as part of moving out, and remind them that the process matters for the future. You will report them to credit bureaus and/or turn them over to a collection company if they don't meet all their financial obligations. The move-out list should include:

   a. Forwarding their mail. Obviously, you want their address for many reasons, including providing you with a new mailing address where you will send their security deposit. Also, the post office has never been known for efficiency. There may be some mail they want to get that didn't get forwarded. We once had about twenty boxes show up at a rental home after the tenant moved out. They did not leave a forwarding address and refused to answer our calls. We called, emailed, texted … nada. The boxes were full of gauze, medical supplies, and tape. After three months we gave up and donated it all to the local free clinic.

    b. Removing all trash, furniture, and personal property.

    c. Leaving the property clean. If they get it professionally cleaned, it must meet your standards. Many say they've done it but don't actually do it. If it doesn't meet your standards, have them send their cleaner back. Then you will see how truthful their claims are.

    d. Paying any outstanding balances. Otherwise, balances may go into collections and on their credit report.

    e. Taking pictures of issues of concern and keeping them until they receive their security deposit or balance owed back.

    f. Reporting any damage they're aware of. That helps provide a better communication chain for repair. However, the tenant should not paint or repair anything without the owner's permission.

5. Access after the official move out should be a NO-NO. We have had folks go back in and have a "farewell party" after they moved out but before they turned over the keys. Document all damage that is not considered preexisting, as well as quotes for the repairs. Use the same inspection process described in chapters 8 and 10.

6. If a dispute arises, go back to the documentation. Documentation is what makes or breaks your case. If you don't have the documentation, you will lose.

Courts have a low tolerance for your opinion.

Let the paper and pictures talk for you.

Unless the tenant is buying a home, they usually need a rental reference. Good companies call or send a form that asks questions about your experience and history with the tenant. Make sure you remind them that you may be asked for a future reference. Many times their behavior keeps them from getting another place. We find many times the more difficult tenants do not seek a reference. They tell the new landlord false information or falsify documents to avoid the new landlord finding out how they behaved during tenancy. When you don't see rent being paid to you, many times they are saving for the rental deposit on a new place.

Avoiding Vacancy

Many times, part of moving them out is showing the property during transition to avoid vacancy. This is *always* a difficult thing to maneuver. Many tenants—happy or unhappy—just see it as a major inconvenience to them.

So here's the nuts and bolts of it. You must have a provision in the lease to be able to enter and show the property, not just for inspections but also for showing to prospective tenants. If you have the provision and you have a good relationship with the tenant, then it may be to your advantage to schedule all the showings in the same one-hour block and offer the tenant a gift card at Starbucks they can use while they are out of the house. If they cooperate with you, then it makes life so much easier. For those who are breaking their lease and need a replacement tenant to fulfill their balance, you usually find the tenant to be very cooperative as they are on the hook and motivated.

Here is the BUT: sometimes it's better to assume the tenant will not have the property in a presentable form until they are entirely out. Or they're the type who will grouch, refuse to leave while you show the property, and say everything that is wrong with the property in front of the prospective new tenant. In that case, just take names of prospective new tenants and wait. Zero vacancy is a wonderful thing, but it takes some mutual collaboration to be successful.

Move Them Out
Key Takeaways

Provide the tenant with clear instructions regarding their move-out responsibilities.

They haven't really moved out until they've turned over the keys.

Documentation is your best friend.

Mutual collaboration can prevent vacancy.

Notes

_____

_____

_____

_____

_____

_____

_____

_____

_____

_____

_____

Take a hard line
and make sure
they understand
you mean business.
**This is, after all,
a business.**

CHAPTER 13

Evict Them

Rogue tenants can leave marks on both your property and your mental wellness. They're double trouble when they take advantage of you *and* treat your property poorly. Many cases of rogue tenants are directly related to property owners "doing property management themselves" and not having the tools or technology to really evaluate the tenant at the very start. Their decision to rent to someone went off a gut reaction to the fact that the tenant "seemed nice" and had the ability to pay—or at least they said they did.

I once had a property manager who used to tell me everyone she met seemed "classy." It's probably true—they did. But like so many things in life, trust but verify. You can easily cut down on evictions in the first place by screening your tenants well as we discussed in chapter 7 and looking under all the necessary rocks. You cannot take someone's word that they are who and what they say they are anymore. But even people with the best intentions and good credentials can have a turn in life that makes a good situation go bad—family issues, breakups, job losses, health issues, you name it. All can contribute to a downhill slide. So what happens when things start to go wrong—what do you do?

First, you have to take a hard line and make sure they understand you mean business. This is, after all, a business. Yes, we are all human, and there is a time for human decency and compassion, but how long are you willing to pay for someone else to live in your home? Many property investors have realized they sacrificed their own families to support other families who in the end really didn't care what had been done for them. The next thing those investors knew, they were the bad guy, and it was all their fault. NOTE: not all evicted tenants are that way, but it's a real trend as personal responsibility is a dying moral characteristic.

Evictions and the process involved are not for the weak of heart (on either side). An older gentleman who owned property once told me he would evict tenants by taking all their stuff out of the house, throwing it in the front yard, and changing the locks. Another person told me he would just take the front door off and throw it into his truck. Ha! That's good to think about for a laugh, but no—that's a no-go. Please don't do either of those unless you want to go to jail and lose way more than a month or two of rent.

The court system is not set up in your favor, so you must first make sure you have followed the laws of your area and have all your ducks in a row. Otherwise, without a doubt, you will lose, and I mean lose every time. You must have a fully executed lease that addresses the terms of the lease, you must give proper notices, and you must have proper documentation of all of those notices. Don't think for one minute that the tenant does not know what they are doing; they absolutely do.

Following are some tips and techniques to think about if you have a tenant who is not performing as intended in the lease and you need a way to get them out of your property as quickly and easily as you can. Remember that eviction laws and processes vary from state to state, so get to know your state's laws.

Note that once you begin the eviction proceedings, you may risk the outcome of your case by taking in some past due rent money from them. North Carolina allows a certain percentage to be paid by the tenant; otherwise, you risk a long delay in your case by taking too much from them during the process. Just know the laws, and if the tenant sends a partial payment that exceeds the percentage, send the money back and do not deposit it. Again, I guarantee they know the rules better than you do.

Legal Process

As our leases are written, the rent is due on the first day of the month. Late fees are applied when they are five or more days late with the payment. If rent is still not in on the fifth day (or they've violated some other terms of the lease), below are the steps we advise you take. Some may vary based on your county, state, or lease terms.

- On the fifth day, call and/or email to ask when rent is coming in and remind them of the late fee. Document your contact (including the date and time if you called) and their response or lack of response.
- On the tenth day, send a letter documenting the delinquency and late fee, even if they said they would be paying you in a couple of weeks.
- If rent payment is still delinquent or if the check hasn't cleared on day eleven to fifteen, file for eviction. This triggers a court date. Remember that you can always cancel it if payment comes through. But if they falter on their commitment, you are already ahead of the process.
- Show up and don't give up. Bring all your documentation (fully executed lease, correspondence, inspections, pictures, and so forth) to court. Be nice to the magistrate and stick to the facts—they don't care about the other stuff. Stick to first-hand accounts unless you have witnesses. Remember that your ultimate goal is to get your property back. The tenant may appeal, but if they do, they may have to pay something to do it (unless they have a hardship claim). The system where you live will dictate some of this.

Some law firms and attorneys specialize in this type of law. *Pay them to handle it for you—it is worth it.* You have a better chance of a positive outcome if you let them guide you and make sure everything is done properly. They manage the court better than us "nasty landlords" who just want our rent and harmony. It's well worth the money.

Work with the tenant if you can—to keep them in the house and/or to recover delinquent payments and damage-repair fees. If you can work it out, and if there are some things that need repair, you can still turn over the delinquent rent and cost for damages to a collection company to handle in some scenarios, which will take the heavy lifting off of you.

Evicting for More Than Just Money

Eviction is often thought of as purely a money issue. If you don't pay, you don't stay, and the court will make it so. That's true for the majority of cases, but there are instances when money is not the focus of the eviction. One of the most common is violating lease provisions regarding terms and conditions of the HOA. It is imperative that your lease protect you in the event you have multiple HOA violations and fines for things such as garbage-can storage, lawn maintenance, prohibited vehicles, prohibited parking, condition of the home and cleanliness—you get the picture. Second, tenants can be evicted for violating other provisions, such as unauthorized pets and occupants that are not approved or a part of the lease without proper notice or authorization.

Proactive Prevention

In my county, you can always start an eviction and cancel it. In your fifth-day and tenth-day communications outlined previously, tell the tenant your plans to report to credit bureaus and agencies that will permanently affect their records. Sometimes just the jolt of having that on their permanent record is enough to snap tenants into shape. For tenants who have hit a bump in the road, consider setting up payment plans. As long as milestones are met and communication is good, it can be worthwhile to work with them and get things on the straight and narrow. There are renters out there who can overcome and do great with a small bit of rent grace. The rest of this chapter concerns the others—the ones who just need to go.

Cash for Keys

Let's say you have a tenant who, up until this point, has been a pretty good tenant. When late, they paid the late fee without complaint. They communicated and did what they said they would do. Everyone was on the same page. But now they have failed their obligation on rent payment according to the lease terms and are even delinquent on the agreed-upon makeup payment plan. And you have given them sufficient notice that they are delinquent as described above.

First, do the obvious: check whether the utilities are still on. If not, they may already be gone. You can also drive by, knock on the door, and see if they are packing. If they are moving, then you know mutually the relationship is over, but the lease remains the link that ties you together.

If the delinquency is not huge, "cash for keys" is a great way to get your property back without the time, cost, and hassle of court. You can cancel an eviction up until the moment you're called up by the magistrate. You just want them out and don't want to run over dollars to pick up dimes. "Cash for keys" goes like this:

1. You and the tenant agree that the tenant will move out by X date and leave the house clean and in good shape.
2. You and the tenant agree they will bring keys to you, and you will inspect the property right then.

3. The tenant agrees to sign a release stating they will have no further claim to the property.

4. You hand the tenant $X for the cost of a moving truck. (I usually do about $400 to $500 if things go as planned.)

If you've started eviction proceedings, and the tenant turns over the keys even without the cash, you should still have them sign a release. If they simply abandon the property, make sure you have a clause in your lease that allows you to take over possession, put on new locks, keep the security deposit, and move on.

When Things Get Ugly

We recently had a very uncooperative tenant who was determined to stay without paying rent, citing numerous issues with the house as their justification for not paying. They were rude and just plain nasty to everyone they spoke to, playing the angry card at every turn and at every conversation.

Threats and bullying are a common tactic we see in rogue tenants. We have a zero-tolerance policy with that kind of behavior and go straight to eviction—do not pass go and do not collect any more of the anger. We then do multiple inspections to make sure the house isn't getting destroyed by an angry tenant. We visit them with notice and document every correspondence and every action. It's the way of the world. Yes, it's hard, but stick to your guns.

By now, we need to say it with feeling: *if they don't pay, they don't stay.* People find it easy to use you as a whipping post for their own shortcomings, but reality has to set in. It's a business, and they are late. The process is clear, so follow it. Remember these rules:

- Do not change the locks.
- Do not shut off the utilities.
- Do not remove their personal property.
- Do not respond to their threats with threats of your own.

If you do any of the above before the court says you can, the rogue tenant has a reason to stay, and the court can delay getting your house back in the near term. It's like a quarterback trying to draw you offsides by shouting in bursts. Provide proper eviction notices and be clear and consistent in your documentation. If you find they don't respond to your notices, post them on their front door and take a picture of it hanging there for your files.

If you find damage, make sure you have your inspection reports (as discussed in chapters 8 and 10) on hand for your court date. This shows you're proactive about the property and helps you prove any of your claims.

When the Sheriff Comes

The sheriff's involvement in eviction varies from state to state. In North Carolina, once the court has determined that you can take back possession of your property, the sheriff will come to perform the official eviction and escort the tenants out. Your locksmith should be there when the sheriff arrives to (1) help the sheriff enter if the tenant is uncooperative and (2) change the locks immediately. Yes, it's hard to see families be locked out, but I implore you to be aware of the following:

- You will need to schedule a convenient time for them to get their stuff out.
- Send someone there to monitor the situation. Don't just open the door and leave.
- Check all windows and make sure they are locked. They might sneak back in and cause issues.
- Get the garage door openers or disconnect the garage door motor. What good is changing the locks if they can enter through garage?
- Talk to neighbors and ask them to call you or the police if the tenants come back. In my state, it is a crime for evicted tenants to reenter property without the landlord or representative

present. Most of the time, neighbors are great allies and the real key to your success. Sometimes they tell you more than you want to know, but it's good to have a set of full-time eyes there.

Identify Your Investment Property
Key Takeaways

Set clear parameters in your lease for what will initiate eviction proceedings.

Avoid evictions with proactive screening and working with tenants who have temporary setbacks.

Each state has a particular legal process for evictions. Follow the process to the letter. Better yet, hire an attorney to help you.

Notes

_____
_____
_____
_____
_____
_____
_____
_____
_____
_____
_____
_____
_____
_____
_____

Reap the benefits

without having to do
all of the work.

CHAPTER 14

Use a Property Management Company

You can absolutely manage your own property and prosper.
But having a property management company on your team will help you reap the benefits without having to do all of the work. Understand two very basic fundamentals: First, they work for you. You call the shots or authorize them to do so. If someone tells you their company is perfect and never makes mistakes, run for the hills. You are dealing with people on all ends, and people do make mistakes, including me. It's how they handle those mistakes and issues that arise that matters. If they handle them with honesty and accountability, then you are on a straight path. Do not think for one second that things will always be smooth, but the minute they are not managing your property effectively, it's time to part ways with them. Second, a vacancy is a gift not a curse. It's not *when* you rent the property but *to whom* you rent it. I have some properties that rent right away and others that take some time to rent, but when they do, it's to the right person at the right time. In the end, that philosophy always makes money, not takes money.

How property management companies work can vary widely because of differing philosophies and differing markets. I will share my company's structure and philosophy to give you a basis of comparison with whomever you may talk to.

How and When Owners Get Paid

We pay property owners on or around the twelfth to fourteenth of the month depending on how the weekend or bank holidays fall. We also do a second check run later in the month for payments that come in late. Note this caveat: remember that we are dealing with trust accounts, so the tenant's payment must first clear the bank. If you're working to establish a property management company, remember that owners always get paid first. Don't make the same mistake that many companies do by catering to yourself before the owner, even if the contract allows it. Owner first, always. We also pay by direct deposit. With all of the check fraud that exists today, direct deposit gives you faster access to your money and reduces risk.

How Property Managers Get Paid

Property management companies charge a variety of fees. You should be aware of what those fees are, who pays them, and what they cover.

- Upfront fee: most management companies charge a percent of rent either at signed lease or move-in. My company charges 50 percent of the first full month's rent. It's a firm-by-firm decision.
- Monthly fee: a percentage of the monthly rent at move-in. Most firms in my area charge 10 percent. Others may charge 8 percent, but it's on a case-by-case basis.
- Late rent fees: this is kept by the management company in most cases. It ranges based on rules for your area. Our area maximum is 5 percent.

- Application fee: this is kept by the management company in most cases and covers fees for databases and other background check tools for eviction, credit, employment, and criminal records.
- Renewal fee: most management companies charge $150 to renew the lease at which time they also look to raise the rent. This is a standard practice for continuation of the lease.
- New tenant turnover fee: when your first tenant moves out and another comes in, many companies repeat the upfront fee. We used to charge 50 percent of the first month's rent, but now we only charge $250. It's a business decision on the management company's part.
- Repair oversight fee: many management companies charge a markup on repairs. We feel that most repairs and management of those repairs fall under management responsibilities, so we shy away from markups unless managing the repairs is overly burdensome. For repairs over $500 where we have to provide heavy oversight, we charge 7 percent on top of the repair invoice and make sure the property owners know well in advance.

Staff

Jamison Property Management is currently set up to manage 500 to 700 properties with the opportunity to expand simply by adding staff. The different roles interact together around goals set by our property owners, and communication revolves around those individual goals. Depending on the staff role, their client may be the property owner, the tenant, or my company's leadership. Here's how we break out the individual roles and responsibilities:

- The owner concierge handles management agreements and communication with the owner around repairs, any tenant issues, or vacancies. That communication continues, of course, until the loop is closed.

- The tenant concierge handles leases and correspondence with the tenant in all phases from beginning to end, including scheduling inspections and handling late payments or evictions.
- The director of first impressions, also known as the office manager, is the first point of contact and answers the phone. They have to be pleasant and patient. They also handle deposits, invoices, mail, and running the office. The tenant concierge reports to this person.
- Property managers are licensed real estate agents who can show property. In our structure, they are salary only; we pay no commission. They work to place tenants for our property owners only and help market and promote those properties. An average property manager can handle around 100 vacancies per year. Applicants may only enter a property when escorted by a licensed agent, no exceptions. Many markets, including ours, have some companies that allow applicants to visit properties unescorted by entering a code on the lock box. This is an absolute nonstarter for me. Let's face it—it's too easy for them to unlock a window and climb back in as a squatter or take the appliances. When you look for a company, make sure it's one that uses a showing agent for your properties, without exception. Agents learn a lot about prospective tenants when they show up face to face.
- The maintenance manager coordinates repairs and routine maintenance, manages vendor relationships (including getting quotes for repairs or work needed), and performs inspections. Depending on our portfolio size at any given time, this person may also hire independent inspectors on a contract basis. We're frequently asked by new property owners how many inspections we perform each year and the cost. We absorb the cost of inspections and perform them two to three times a year unless conditions require otherwise. Our vendors also act as additional eyes and ears, so we have them look for things when we do routine HVAC or other needed maintenance.

Concierge-Level Service Structure

Most property management companies communicate with property owners in writing. The software we use allows us to send and document written communications and mobile text messages inside the system. But I am old fashioned. I have my staff follow up all written communication with a good ol' phone call to avoid any misunderstandings. I mean, we are talking about a very expensive asset here, a house to you and a home to others, right? The software, although not human, is collaborative with human intervention and provides a complete suite of tools for all the job descriptions above.

Tenant Screening

We screen all applicants on behalf of our clients. That includes:

- Verifying income
- Verifying employment with a phone call to the employer
- Contacting past landlords and asking them to complete a questionnaire about the tenant's history
- Completing a criminal background and sex-offense check
- Searching nationally for any past evictions
- Running the credit check

We look for income three times the rent, no past evictions, no sex offenses or other criminal convictions that could endanger other tenants, and a credit score greater than 540.

Leases

Make sure the property management company's standard lease is attorney approved. We use the standard North Carolina Real Estate Commission and North Carolina Bar Association approved forms plus addendums written by our attorneys for various issues including bed bugs, smoking, social media, drugs, and spices.

Selling Your Property

If we are managing your property and you decide to sell it to your tenant, since we procured that tenant, we are entitled to a 6 percent sales commission unless you specify a different Realtor®. The property management contract can specify your outside Realtor's name (or your name if you're a licensed Realtor®) and give them first right of refusal for that listing if you ever wish to sell. We give Realtors® clear pathways to refer managed properties to us. We like to keep options open for landlords and agents who don't want to lose clients by referring them to our property management company.

How to Start a Property Management Company

Start with managing your own property. No one in the business that I know of has any level of success if they don't first know how to walk in the shoes of an investor. As we have a fiduciary duty to them and certainly a duty to serve the tenant, we must stand in the shoes of the investor to truly understand where they are. When I was an investor with a management company helping me, I learned a lot about what I did not want. Their objectives and continued fees and costs drove me away from their self-serving business model and into my own business—a blessing in disguise.

Next, look for one of my speaking engagements or hang on for my next book, which will go into more detail on how to start your own property management company. This book is a great basis for many aspects of the business, but it's more of a broad overview. If, like me, you find yourself here unintentionally but blessed to be on the journey to having investment property, read and study all you can. The startup pathway can be very difficult until you realize the key to success is finding good people to make it really work out and not doing it all yourself. If you expect to climb financially quickly, you will be disappointed quickly.

Use a Property Management Company
Key Takeaways

Your property management company works for you, not the other way around. Interview them and ask questions before you hire them.

Their fees should come out of the rental income for managing the property. You shouldn't have to pay them over and above that unless you need them to supervise expensive repairs.

Become a property investor before attempting to start a property management company where you manage other peoples' investments. You must be in an investor's shoes first.

Notes

You'll need
a solid team

of people
who are close
to the rental.

CHAPTER 15

Vacation for Fun and Profit

When you buy an investment home, you must remove yourself emotionally from the process and make sure your tastes aren't interfering with the decision. I have had many investors take on fits of gagging at the sight of a home's countertops, but in the eyes of the tenant who would be living there, those countertops are perfectly acceptable and commonplace. There are some universal common updates, like paint and flooring, but for the most part, you must focus on renters' wants and needs, not your own.

In the evaluation and décor category, vacation rentals are a different story. I wrote most of this book from my family's oceanfront vacation home in South Carolina. I like to stare at the ocean to gather my thoughts. It's such a peaceful place for clarity and introspection. If you plan to use the property for some personal use (check the IRS definition of what qualifies as "some"), it's time to take a look at the emotional side of the investment purchase. Ask yourself: Where do I want to vacation? Why do I love it there? What do I do when I'm there? What are some external costs for items other than meals when I'm there? What's missing from the place where I stay now? What would children do if it rains or even during the day? What is different about my place to make it unique?

Picking Your Where

Obviously, where you decide to purchase a vacation property is a very personal decision with criteria ranging from completely irrational to your own likes and desires. Many people want to buy where they went as children and have fond family memories. Others go for an experience. Of course, just because you like to vacation in a particular place does not mean it's a great investment location. But we'll proceed under the premise that other people love the same vacation locations that you do.

For the sake of our example, let's consider the most common denominators of vacation rentals. The ocean is a biggie—the beach draws the largest crowd from families to snowbirds. Most places along the coast will have a season that depends, of course, on the weather and amenities available. Consider these questions when choosing your where: When do most people go? When is the weather best? What are the fun things to do in the area? Are the amenities within walking distance, biking distance, or driving distance? Can you ride bikes safely? Is it kid friendly? How far away is the food, both dining and grocery? Now replace the word "ocean" with amusement park, ski resort, mountain retreat, and hiking, and all the same questions apply.

The properties that seem to work the best are in areas that provide a unique experience to families or certain age groups. Communities geared toward the silver generation but with room to accommodate grandchildren stand apart in the current economy and generation mix. Today, family vacations seem to include not just immediate family but also extended family (mostly all the parents and grandparents). Warmer climates or coastal climates have year-round appeal. In our beachfront home in the Carolinas, we see many Canadians and others escaping severe winter conditions up north and seeking milder temperatures, even though they are not optimal for sunbathing. They always say mid 50s beats -50 any day.

The farther away the vacation rental is from where you live, the more concerns you should have about the opportunity. For example, my wife wants to purchase a place in Hawaii. Personally, I really love Hawaii, but it is such a chore to get there, and I just don't want to put myself in a position where I can't control any of the outcomes. But to each his own. I think a four- to five-hour limit on driving is a good rule of thumb. If you simply are not that close to your ideal property, at least establish some flight or driving parameters to help in your decision process. You never know when the absolute need to get there could arise or a weekend escape just has to happen to maintain sanity.

Picking Your Realtor®

Even though I am a Realtor®, I know I need help when I buy homes outside my area of expertise. There are so many important things to know about an area that only an expert in the market will know. So if you are a Realtor® or if you consider yourself an expert researcher, please put your ego aside and get help. Yes, websites provide tons of data and information about areas and investment property, but let's put this on the table early: not everything you read on the Internet is the truth; and people who sell primary homes aren't necessarily good at investment property analysis and identification based on your goals and desired personal and financial outcomes.

When looking for a Realtor® for investment properties, ask these strategic questions:

1. Do you live in the area you are recommending?
2. How many investment properties do you own or have you sold in the last couple of years?
3. How long have you been in the business?
4. Do you specialize in a type of investment property?
5. Do you know about any trends that will improve or degrade the area you are recommending?

6. Can you provide me with rental projections and returns?
7. Do you have a lender that specializes in these types of investments?
8. Do you "have a guy" or gal to help with maintenance? (See chapter 11.)
9. May I have references?
10. Do you have a management company you use, or do you think self-management makes more sense in this case?
11. How many people like me are you working with right now?
12. Do you have some investors you have worked with that would be interested in selling?

Everyone has to get experience by being hands-on. Every Realtor® and investor learns and makes mistakes when buying, owning, and managing property—those are the lessons that stay with you because you feel every one of them intimately. But you don't have to wing it. Get an experienced Realtor® mentor, or if you have a friend who has invested in the area, let their mistakes become your first steps to success. In short, work with an expert who has done this multiple times to help guide you for your first few purchases.

When buying, in most cases, the seller pays for the Realtor's® time, and even if they don't, pay a good Realtor® for the experience of not getting trapped. Take a hard look at the list above and don't fall into the trap of calling into an agency and whoever is on phone duty that day becomes your Realtor®. Experienced agents don't do phone duty. (Sorry, phone duty agents.) You have to dig to get the one who can best guide you. Many people in this business get a ton of flack for driving nice cars and being successful, but most did not get there overnight; it was a long road, and they have experience you really need. I have been in situations where I have been out four to five times with investors before we found the right home. If your Realtor® needs the sale to eat versus doing what is best for you, they're coming from a place of desperation not contribution. Certainly they want to make money, but they also need to be patient along with you.

Personality and the ability to have frank conversations are also critical to this relationship, so you better get along with your agent. You don't want to waste their time, nor should they waste yours. If you are not ready to buy and are just exploring, tell them up front. Don't run them ragged for the opportunity to kick tires when you're not ready to pull the trigger on something. Get someone in the heart of where you want to be and be patient because the right one is out there. And if you can't find a Realtor®, be sure to find an investor, as I said earlier, in the area to lean on and show you the ins and outs of the area in the same way.

Assemble the Rest of Your Team

Since your vacation rental is likely far from where you live, you'll need a solid team of people who are close to the rental and who can jump on issues as quickly as you would. If you're working with the right Realtor® or property management company, they can help you create this team. I would also argue that you need this team in your corner before you even start looking for property.

A "Guy"

Remember our guy (or gal) from chapter 11? He or she is even more important for your vacation rental. You must have someone close by to handle things when you are not there. It is the most critical piece to the puzzle. If you don't "have a guy," you better be close enough to get there in a moment's notice. This person is a true know-it-all in the best sense of the word. They know everyone and everything there is to know and how to find someone at a moment's notice to get any—and I mean *any*—job done. When you find your guy, treat them like royalty. Spoil them rotten. It's worth it.

My guy at the coast was named Hutch. He was like the mayor of the island. He knew everyone, and everyone knew him. He was handy as could be, could fix anything, and knew every piece of news coming and going on the island. If you needed something done, he had an endless supply of resources in his head to choose from and wouldn't nickel and dime you to death. When Hutch left the island, he passed me on to his network. He shared his treasure chest with his blessing and kept things going for us.

If you don't have a Hutch, then speak to your Realtor® or other homeowners in the area to find one. They are always there—you just have to find them. If they answer their phone and actually show up, you are 90 percent of the way there. Just make sure your guy has a heart to be helpful and isn't always referring you to their out-of-work family members for repair issues and stuffing their pockets at your expense.

Cleaning Crew

Another linchpin to success in vacation rentals is your cleaning crew. When you get a good one that also answers their phone and shows up on time, you have to keep them happy. You'll have many different people coming into your home with different levels and expectations of what "clean" means. Let's face it—there are some people in this world you will never ever satisfy. So you will need someone who, at a moment's notice, can show up and be ready to clean up any tiny things to make your renter happy. The anchor of most bad reviews on social media has to do with cleanliness or owner communication. These are the two biggies. When problems happen, being available and helpful will always overcome any issue that arises. Nothing is worse than being on vacation and being stuck with no lifeline.

We keep our cleaner incentivized by offering them a bonus if they help us maintain a five-star rating on review sites. If you get no complaints, you can give them an extra bonus for every third or fourth renter. This makes them take even more care. Recognition is just as key as the money. If they realize they are in this with you (and the right cleaner will), they should share in your success. Make sure you pay for each cleaning as people check out. To keep things in the present, do not pay in advance.

Handyman

If your "guy" isn't also a handyman with a general knowledge of fixing things around the house, you'll need a good handyman you can trust. Again, your Realtor® should have a stable group of people you can call to come to the rescue any time of day. Most of the time it's simple stuff, but many times just when you have an easy call to change a bulb or handle a beeping smoke detector, a pipe bursts or the A/C goes out. The worst is the refrigerator quitting with all their vacation food in it. Always ask other owners whom they use. This is a tough spot to fill. Keep a deep bench of options as sometimes you may have a scheduling issue and need to call on your backup or backups for help.

Pest Control Company

Bugs happen; it's a part of this business. Put a good pest control company on contract, so they come whenever for whatever. It's a necessary thing. Keep it regular and make sure they guarantee their work. Ours says if you see something moving, call.

HVAC

Get recommendations for a local company that is well staffed and highly responsive. I have two, the local guy and a larger regional company. HVAC issues can make or break your summer resort business. No one likes to be out in the cold either. Get their cell number or an emergency phone number. It may not seem like an emergency to you, but for people on vacation, everything is an emergency, and most people leave their brains at home. I have two on call at all times. When it's hot at home, it's usually *really hot* at the coast.

Evaluating Potential Property

One of my best lessons learned when I began to look at vacation rentals was to find features that either were in short supply or brought a level of convenience that made the property more unique. When I was investing in Florida, one of our units was on the main floor and offered just a short walk to the ocean. Not that it wasn't great to be higher up, but the rentals for this unit were off the hook with elderly folk not having to do steps—just a quick, easy walk outside to the ocean. Access is an asset; it was more important to a certain audience than the view in many instances. Having a wheelchair-accessible property is also great. This allows families to bring elderly parents or others with disabilities. It is a great option to really set you apart.

Another great lesson is to understand the word "view." Not all homes have views, so a good view is a key piece of the puzzle. Of course, the more unique the view, the more unique the property and the more stable the investment regardless of economic conditions. But I want to be clear here: a real view is my point. Not a tip-toe view. A real, bona fide view where you can see the desired scenery without having to strain or have all the leaves off the trees.

Access to amenities is another differentiator to consider. If you can see or be near the pool or other amenities, it plays well in rentals. Location, location, location—look for the things about the unit that make it unique and different from sunrise to sunset.

All of the features aside, before you buy, get a clear understanding of how rentals perform in the area and how much rental income you will need to either break even or make a profit. Rental sites are the greatest asset for this research. Act as a potential guest and research properties, locations, and property types and their various rental rates. Look at their calendars to see their "seasons of success" and how rates vary based on weather conditions or times of year. When I was looking at my family's first vacation property, I developed a very conservative pro forma gradually increasing rents over time for repeat renters and getting established.

You don't need to be an accountant; it's just simple math to calculate a break-even point, so you know how many weeks of rental you need annually. In the following example, I need the home rented for thirty-three weeks each year to break even. Don't work off of "soft dollars" in this analysis, such as asset depreciation or other tax related write-offs. Just work on the basic costs first.

Potential Rent				
Season	# Weeks	Rate/ Week	Total	Expenses Charged to Guest*
Spring	8	$1,500	$12,000	$600
Summer	12	$2,000	$24,000	$1,000
Fall	8	$1,500	$12,000	$600
Winter	5	$1,000	$5,000	$300
Total Annual Income Potential	**33**		**$53,000**	**$2,500**

* Sales tax, parking fees, bicycle rentals, cleaning fees, and so forth

Expenses	
Insurance	$1,500
Maintenance	$2,500
Maintenance Reserves	$2,500
Mortgage Payment P&I	$24,000
HOA Fees	$6,000
Property Taxes	$3,000
Cleaning	$3,000
Management Fees	$8,200
Replacing Broken/Misplaced Items	$1,000
Marketing	$1,000
Total Expenses	**$52,700**

As you can see above, the management fee is a huge part of your calculation. Know your costs, don't under- or overestimate, and don't move into analysis paralysis.

The HOA is also an important factor to consider. Being a part of an HOA makes many people cringe, but when it comes to your vacation property, I think it's an advantage. The consistency and oversight that an HOA offers aesthetically is key to the desirability of the location. They also have rules and restrictions that keep things in good working order. Note, however, that many HOAs limit rentals, so you better be darn sure the unit you buy can be rented for the periods you need to make the numbers work. There are also lending restrictions in some units where a building is only allowed to have a certain percentage of rentals according to the complex lending limits or neighborhood HOA covenants and restrictions. Also, there may be other restrictions for rentals causing them not to be eligible for preferred financing. I know someone who bought a unit unaware that the minimum term for rentals in the complex was three months. *Make sure you or your Realtor® are clear on the HOA rules and whether the rules fit with the type of rental and renter you need for a return on your investment. This is critical!*

Contracts

Make sure you have a contract for your guests to dictate rules and cover liability in your vacation rental. It should spell out who will be in your home, when they can get in, when they check out, and other expectations. Most importantly, it should protect you from liability if they fall down or do something stupid. Remember that on vacation many people leave their brains at home letting loose of common sense and responsibility—it's amazing but true. In the appendix, you will find an example of my agreement, but don't use this one—get an attorney to tailor one to your circumstances. Make sure it covers these items:

- Their name and contact information
- Address of the property
- Dates of the stay
- Costs, including when they are due and totals

- Damage insurance and their liability for damage
- What happens if damages occur
- Your address to return the *signed* contract and payment instructions
- Cancellation policy
- Pet policy
- Smoking policy
- Check-in and check-out times
- Rules for parking and the HOA
- Handy tips like when garbage is picked up and how to dispose of it
- How they are to leave the unit, including notes on what to do with trash, laundry, and leftover food
- Notes on what happens if they don't follow rules
- Waiver releasing you from any and all liabilities

Make sure it also has lines for initials and signatures and be sure to get it back before they stay in your vacation rental. It's a must have. Don't send them the door codes or set up parking for them until you get a signed contract and full payment.

Make Your Property Rent-Ready

Much of the information in chapter 4 applies here as well. There are a few key differences though.

- Avoid keys. Instead, use coded, battery-operated electric locks and then send renters the code when their reservation is confirmed. You could even install a smart lock you can control from your phone or computer. That means you can give repair people temporary passcodes to get in when needed and delete the code once the job is complete.
- Install a smart thermostat you can control from your phone. Sometimes people crank up the temperature and then leave it when they check out. It will pay for itself quickly.

- Place TV and cable instructions in handy spots and make more than one copy. They tend to get lost or thrown away.
- Put laminated or framed house rules on the wall for all to see. Don't expect them to follow your rules if you don't make everyone aware what they are.
- Don't install a phone. Let them use their mobile phones.
- Put deadbolts on the owner's cabinets to protect your personal belongings. Bored children frequently try to break into owners' cabinets and often succeed. Deadbolts are more challenging and eliminate the ability to use a credit card to gain entry.
- Change batteries in your smoke and CO detectors and thermostat often. As luck would usually have it, the batteries in those devices usually like to die and start beeping at 2 a.m.
- Stock the home with spare filters, batteries, and bulbs for guests.

Making Your Rental Stand Out

Let's say you don't have the great view or ideal location. What can you do to make the unit unique and set it apart? This requires some thought about how you would spend your time or how your target audience would spend their time. Even a one-bedroom home can be as unique and appealing as a four-plus bedroom home. Following are some examples of things to think about adding or including.

- Many people who come cannot unplug from work. Provide a work station in the unit with great Internet and a printer and scanner.
- Provide video games like a Wii. We always thought the games were for the kids until we had a group of senior ladies enjoying a girls' weekend in one of our rentals that has a game station. We have a game in our library of DVDs, VCR tapes, and games called *Let's Dance*. Those women drank some adult beverages, danced every night, and just had a ball.

- Provide golf carts and/or bikes to use. This one can be a blessing and a curse, but let's look at rationale. During vacation season at one of our homes, renting bikes and carts from the rental company is $700 for a week. That is a tremendous expense on top of the cost of the rental (about 35 percent more). We provide four bikes and two carts. We found when you have more than three people staying at a home, they may not always want to do the same thing. But they also may want to go somewhere without having to make two trips, so having two carts was a real game changer to our rental experience, and everyone wanted one. Be ready, though, because there are some unforeseen costs to keep bikes and carts well maintained. Those things break. Salt and sea air are not kind to them.
- Get over-the-top TV and cable service. Make them never want to go home.
- Buy towels and sheets of superior quality, but make sure you choose dark colors. White is a poor choice in a vacation rental. Bleach kills towels. And how often have you had to sleep on sandpaper sheets in a rental? Give them a reason to come back. We chose towels that were dark. The colors best suited for rentals are brown and dark blue. We also kept backup white towels for those who use personal care products with benzoyl peroxide or other chemicals that will ruin colored towels.
- Allow pets, *within limits.* Many people want to take their dogs on vacation. Provide a crate and a clear set of rules, and you will gain more renters since most rentals are not pet friendly. Have a refundable pet deposit of at least $300 to cover potential damage. Be clear on the breed and size restrictions and provide an extra-large crate to accommodate any sized dog—if they are driving, it is a waste of car space to bring their own. And be clear that pets are not allowed on the furniture or beds even if you have plastic liners on your mattresses. Be clear as to where the dog does its business

and provide tools to clean things up. Don't allow cats—sorry, too many hair, allergy and urine issues. Make sure your carpet pad has a moisture barrier—take no chances on urine getting into the carpet pad. Once there, it never comes out.

- Alternatively, don't ever allow pets. Many other people like that. It gives them reassurance that they don't have to deal with any dander or pet odor issues.
- Good appliances, coffee makers, and wine coolers give the perception of top shelf.
- Furnishings are a big deal. A couple years ago, we rented a location in Florida that had an ocean view and a screen porch with a fabulous sunset view. But the furniture was very old and dated with flower prints. It was not "beachy," and it looked like they took old furniture from their house and brought it to the rental. Don't do this. You can decorate to many styles; don't just use your hand-me-down décor. It's a vacation, not a place to store your grandma's old stuff.

When Issues Arise

You really see the strength of your "guy" and cleaning crew when issues arise. If they respond quickly and without drama, you are truly on a path to success. But there is a key here that can dilute those partnerships—you or your management company. *"What? Me?!"* you say. Let's be clear—if you do not respond in a timely manner to their issues or your management company does not offer any type of after-hours response, your future success is really at risk.

When people are on vacation, they have very high expectations of quick responses. This is the absolute truth. If my renters call or text me, I am back to them at that moment. Responsiveness makes a huge difference in having repeat customers versus one-time guests.

An extreme case: many years ago, we had a guest checking into one of our homes. We had just left the home a few weeks earlier and spent thousands of dollars on new beds and bedding in many of the rooms. At 10 p.m., I received a text that said, "You deceived me. I was under the understanding that all the beds and bedding were new, and the master bedroom mattress is stained." I went back to our website, and it said "many new beds and bedding in the house." Yes, that's a little vague. Truth be told, they were all new beds, and in all rooms but the master, there were also new mattresses.

I tried multiple times to call back, and the guest did not answer. I lay in bed worried and a mess. The way I heard it, she was basically calling me a liar and a cheat. I would not stand for that and would go to any length to protect my integrity and make things right. So I got up at 5 a.m. and told my wife I was headed to the beach house. She was floored, but you know what? She decided to come along. I knew if I left right then, I would arrive when the furniture store opened and could buy new mattresses for that last bedroom. I grabbed our company truck to bring them straight to the house—brand new, unslept on, and ready. I was determined to do whatever was needed and whatever it took to make them happy. So I waited until about 8:30 a.m. when well en route and sent the guest a text to let her know my plan and that I was well on the way. Immediately, she called and said, "Oh, I am sorry. We were just tired. I didn't mean it." Well, you know that inspired me even more. I told her, "I am on my way. I will be there at noon with new mattresses," because no one would ever call me a liar or deceiver.

I arrived with a new mattress, and when I went into the master bedroom and pulled back the sheets in the master bedroom, the mattress was absolutely flawless. She was, yes, "one of those," but I replaced it anyway. After her continued embarrassment over her behavior, I learned another lesson: how you react and the battles you pick are important, which is true not in just this case but also in life. People don't always act like they should, but how you react can make or break any situation. In my head, I wanted to scream at her, but I did not. I took the high road. Funny, she left some of their personal belongings behind by mistake and took a golf cart key home. Again, I took the high road, but when she asked to come back the next year, I gave her a no-go, thank you very much, and bye-bye.

Beware that some renters will complain in order to get discounts from you. You will learn that people will pick on things, so you have to be ready to combat that by checking in on them and asking what you can do to make sure they have a five-star experience at the beginning, middle, and end of their stay. If you check in, you are able to head off some issues they might not mention until the end of the trip, when you can't resolve anything, and then give you a sucky review. Check in; it makes perfect sense.

Marketing Your Property

If you use a property manager, they should handle marketing for you. But it's interesting that some only use their own proprietary websites to list your property. I don't recommend using those particular property managers. But if you have to, make sure you have an agreement that you can list the property on other websites, and if you get a rental from your listing, you get reduced property management fees for being the procuring cause. I have taken the information from where my guests come from and have done some selective marketing to those areas or used some keywords focused in that geographic area to get more exposure.

Websites are by far the best venue to advertise and the easiest to show the most information to the greatest number of people. I use HomeAway and VRBO (Vacation Rental by Owner). There are so many choices. As part of your evaluation before you buy the property, you will see what comes up in searches for vacation rentals in those areas. See which ones seem to offer the best information and are most user friendly. Stay away from free sites like Craigslist. You want to be a part of a reputable site that offers good visibility. You get what you pay for.

Another great idea is to print something up for the local real estate offices, not just your own Realtor® though. When they have clients come to town to view properties, you may get a rental or two from them. Truly you need to think outside the box. If it is a resort area, residents may need to bunk guests in rentals when they don't have enough room in their own homes. Think about other places where you can post your information to attract potential guests. Talk to wedding and event planners. Talk to the local chamber of commerce. Talk to different restaurants that may let you put something up or have contacts looking for a place to stay. If you have time, create your own website and Facebook page. Try Google AdWords to increase your website's visibility. Honestly though, happy guests are your best marketing tool. And that brings me to reviews.

Reviews

Vacation rentals live and die on reviews. If you have negative reviews, you will lose your standing and income. Airbnb and other sites all know that potential guests want to stay at a location with five-star reviews—vacationers don't want trouble. At least now some of the sites allow you to rate the guests too. This helps you avoid guests who are trouble. I love this; it's about equal time.

Many times people will critique you for things you absolutely have no control over. Or you may have people you cannot ever make happy no matter how hard you try. I recently had a guest give me a four-star review—the first I had gotten in years. So I called her and asked what happened that she felt the home didn't meet her expectations. She said that the weather did not cooperate and that the restaurant on the island gave her bad service. Oh, man, at first the little voice in my brain wanted to scream. I politely asked her to do me a favor and remember that she was evaluating my home, not the weather or restaurants, and asked her to review the restaurant separately, which she did.

When people look for a place to stay, they naturally gravitate to the highest reviews. It's just human nature, and they believe whatever is said regardless of the other side of the circumstances. In another extreme case, I had a woman crash my golf cart into a wall. Yes, she was drunk and admitted it and paid for the repair, but she gave me a lower rating. I could not believe she did that, but it does happen that some people put their misadventures on your shoulders. That is when I learned the following technique.

1. Call them just after they arrive and ask if everything is OK. Tell them you want them to have a five-star experience and to call if anything is out of place. If you aren't close by, give them the number of "your guy." Make sure your management company has those policies in place too.

2. Call in the middle of their stay and ask. "How are things going? Any questions? Anything we can do to make the remaining part of your stay a five-star experience?" If it's something you can do, do it.

3. When they leave, call and ask how their stay was. Tell them you hope they had a five-star experience and thank them for staying with you.

These three touches help you to ensure you address any issues they maybe/could/might/will have, and if you know about them, you can do something about it. If they do have an issue, resolve it quickly or offer a small concession of a gift card for the inconvenience. People sometimes really just want to be heard, and it's your chance to let them be "helpful" and make their suggestions, even if they are not really helpful.

A big part of the review is how you respond to issues. Sound familiar? If you look at my reviews, one thing you will see over and over is "owner was very responsive." They love that. Call them back or text them—it makes a huge difference.

Deals

Vacation rentals always get inquiries for "deals." You would not believe some of the deals people have asked for. One person asked to let them stay for free for a month, and in exchange, they would take some photos of the property for my website. Oh, it gets better. One wanted to paint the house in exchange for 50 percent off the rent, so they could afford to pay for their child's wedding. The list goes on and on. OK, one more: they wanted me to give them $500 off, so they could get their car fixed.

So here is my policy: our differentiators, which they would pay for above and beyond the rental that we provide them, are the deal. I tell them that renting carts and bikes separately would cost over $700. That usually does it. Other than that, the only "deals" I ever offer are to my repeat guests or active military.

Repeat Guests

Keep a list of your naughty and nice guests. Just like relatives, you try and make sure you don't invite the problem children back again. But we *love* repeat guests, especially those who make the rental a family tradition. They come back and treat the place great, and you know and they know what to expect. I send out a note annually thanking them, and I also offer a small token if they book early. Make them feel special. Here are a few ideas:

- Restaurant gift card
- Bottle of wine
- Handwritten note
- Small discount on rent
- Welcome gift basket

Vacation for Fun and Profit
Key Takeaways

Balance the emotional side of a vacation home with the analytic side of an investment property. Run your numbers to find your break-even point.

Get a great local team in place to be there when you can't.

Reviews are everything. Use great communication to make sure your guests have five-star experiences.

Notes

Downloadable Resources

The tools on the following pages are available for download at pauljamison.com/downloads. Use the password **OiKpJDoNe** to access them. The downloadable versions may be more up to date and may differ from the samples that appear in the book. These are to be used purely as guides. We ask that you not share them but use them to benefit your success.

GETTING STARTED SPREADSHEET

To get organized at the beginning of your search, color code the different properties based on your search criteria. This gives you a good overview to determine if the property will even make the final evaluation list.

Jamison!
PROPERTY MANAGEMENT

NMLS #	Address	Zip Code	Subdivision	Yr. Built
3509093	6719 Paloverde Lane, Charlotte, NC	28227	Hickory Ridge	1979
3508018	9515 Long Hill Drive, Charlotte, NC	28214	Riverbend	2006
3511381	6322 Martin Lake Road, Charlotte, NC	28227	Martin Lakes	1988
3478010	7813 Pawtuckett Road, Charlotte, NC	28214	Forest Pawtuckett	1974
3512024	8608 Fallsdale Drive, Charlotte, NC	28214	Coulwood	1968
3512192	103 W Bank Drive, Charlotte, NC	28214	Coulwood	1991
3511475	1662 Midbrook Drive, Rock Hill, SC	29732	Oakwood Acres	1991
3498367	790 Wofford Street, Rock Hill, SC	29730	Harrell Estates	1979
3502766	612 Bancroft Drive, Rock Hill,SC	29730	Winthrop Estates	1963
3510317	721 Golden Bell Drive, Rock Hill, SC	29732	Brittany Meadows	2000
3497985	1268 Christopher Circle, Rock Hill, SC	29730	Spencer Estates	1966
3505388	732 Norwood Avenue, Rock Hill, SC	29730	Sedgefield	1962
3512390	801 Painted Lady Court, Rock Hill, SC	29732	Boatshore	2004
3511013	21 Linestowe Drive, Belmont, NC	28012	Aberfoyle	1924
3512628	109 Juanita Drive, Pineville, NC	28134	Franklin Park	1973
3512754	3021 Old House Circle, Matthews, NC	28105	Thompson Plant	1989
3511695	7902 Teakwood Road, Indian Trail, NC	28079	Hemby Acres	1975
3412672	6700 Mimosa Street, Indian Trail, NC	28079	Lake Park	2001
3510570	6204 Mapleleaf Drive, Indian Trail, NC	28079	Beacon Hill	1978
3487134	1009 Ridgefield Circle, Indian Trail, NC	28079	Ridgefield	1994
3509360	7733 Davis Road, Mint Hill, NC	28227	Timber Creek	1975
3510971	2311 River Chase Drive, Monroe, NC	28110	River Chase	1997
3511938	4319 Red Hook Road, Monroe, NC	28110	St. Johns Forest	2005
3509310	4525 Marshall Court, Monroe, NC	28110	Myers Meadows	2005

Coming Soon

Rock Hill/Pineville

For the Next Run

Other Showings in the PM

PROPERTY INVESTMENT ANALYSIS

(Worksheet 1 - Pro Forma)

Client Name: Jane Doe
Property Address: 123 Main Street, City, State 12345

Jamison!
PROPERTY | DONE™
INVESTMENTS

List Price of Property	$199,900	
Fair Market Value	$190,000	
Discount (%,$)	0%	$10,000
Purchase Price	$190,000	
Percent Down	50%	
Down Payment Amount	$95,000	
Amount of Loan	$95,000	
Interest Rate	5.50%	
Costs of Repairs (Make Ready)	$15,000	
Length of Mortgage (Years)	30	
Payment	Monthly	Annual
Monthly Mortgage Payment	$539.40	$6,472.79

Rental Income	Monthly	Annual
Unit A	$1,400.00	$16,800.00
Unit B	$-	$-
Unit C	$-	$-
Unit D	$-	$-
Gross Rental Income	$1,400.00	$16,800.00
Vacancy Rate	5%	
Net Rental Income	**$1,330.00**	**$15,960.00**

Expenses	Monthly	Annual
Property Management Fees	$140.00	$-
Leasing Costs	$-	$850.00
Maintenance Reserve	$150.00	$100.00
Utilities	$-	$-
Property Taxes	$175.00	$
Insurance	$80.00	$
Misc. (HOA fees, Lawn Care, Trash, etc)	$-	$
Total Expenses	**$545.00**	**$950.00**

Expenses & Vacancy as
% of Gross Rental Income
10.65%

Net Operating Income	**$785.00**	**$15,010.00**

Mortgage Payment	$539.40	$6,472.79
Total Cash In (Downpayment + Repairs)	$110,000.00	
Net Cash Flow	**$245.60**	**$8,537.21**

Investment Analysis	
Appreciation Rate (20 YR AVG = 4.4%)	4.4%
Rent Appreciation (20 YR AVG = 3.1%)	3.1%
Cost to Sell Property	6.0%

PROPERTY INVESTMENT ANALYSIS

(Worksheet 2 - ROI Analysis)

If you use leverage, look at your cash-on-cash return. It's a long-term investment followed by the value of using your money versus someone else's. Look at the whole picture and your goals to determine what return to shoot for. I like at least 8 percent on my cash, but I'm willing to sacrifice some return parameters for a better long-term gain.

Investment Return over Time

Jamison!
PROPERTY INVESTMENTS | DONE™

Year	Gross Rents (Adjusted for Inflation)	Rent Appreciation Rate	Vacancy	Net Rental Income (Annual)	Annual Expenses (Adjusted for Inflation)	Total ROI (Annual)	Cash on Cash ROR (Annual)
1	$16,800	3.1%	5%	$15,960	$950	17%	8%
2	$17,321	3.1%	5%	$16,455	$976	17%	8%
3	$17,858	3.1%	5%	$16,965	$1,002	18%	9%
4	$18,411	3.1%	5%	$17,491	$1,029	19%	9%
5	$18,982	3.1%	5%	$18,033	$1,057	20%	10%
6	$19,571	3.1%	5%	$18,592	$1,085	21%	10%
7	$20,177	3.1%	5%	$19,168	$1,115	22%	11%
8	$20,803	3.1%	5%	$19,763	$1,145	23%	11%
9	$21,448	3.1%	5%	$20,375	$1,176	24%	12%
10	$22,112	3.1%	5%	$21,007	$1,207	5%	12%
11	$22,798	3.1%	5%	$21,658	$1,240	%	13%
12	$23,505	3.1%	5%	$22,329	$1,273	5	13%
13	$24,233	3.1%	5%	$23,022	$1,308		14%
14	$24,985	3.1%	5%	$23,735	$1,343		14%
15	$25,759	3.1%	5%	$24,471	$1,379		15%
16	$26,558	3.1%	5%	$25,230	$1,417		16%
17	$27,381	3.1%	5%	$26,012	$1,455		16%
18	$28,230	3.1%	5%	$26,818	$1,494		17%
19	$29,105	3.1%	5%	$27,650	$1,535		18%
20	$30,007	3.1%	5%	$28,507	$1,576		19%
21	$30,937	3.1%	5%	$29,390	$1,619		19%

Dear Tenants,

Congratulations! Your lease application has been approved for Address, Charlotte, NC 28227.

Your move-in date will be **January 25th, 2019**. The security deposit is $1,398.00 and the monthly rent will be $1,398.00.

The monthly rental rate is part of our discounted rent program, so that if rent is paid on or before the 5th of the month, rent is $1,398.00 per month. If rent is paid after the 5th, rent will be the non-discounted rate of $1,498.00; **this is stated in section 28C of the lease.**

Attached is the Tenant Welcome Package and Rental Policies; please be sure to read it, sign the back page and return to us upon move-in.

Also attached is the Reservation Form. We will need the signed form and the **$250.00 within 2 days** to secure the property. This amount will be credited towards your first rent.

The following move-in items will need verification before move-in is complete:

1. Contact the Utility companies (Electric, Gas, Water) to have service placed in your name.

2. Secure a Renters Insurance Policy with $100,000.00 personal liability coverage and add Jamison Property Management as additional interest.

The following payments* need to be paid to Jamison Property Management BEFORE MOVE-IN DAY:

1. $1,398.00 = for the Security Deposit

2. $1,474.20 = Pro-rated January Rent + February Rent – Reservation Fee

* These payments must be in the form of **CERTIFIED FUNDS** (certified cashier's check or money order <u>only</u>).
* They must be paid/written as **<u>SEPARATE</u>** checks or money orders, payable to JAMISON PROPERTY MANAGEMENT.

Once the reservation fee is received, the lease will be prepared and sent by email, for your electronic signatures.

Please contact our office if you have any questions.

Jamison Property Management
500 W John St, Matthews, NC 28105
Phone: 704-846-3663
Fax: 704-847-3663

MOVE-IN INSPECTION FORM

MOVE-IN INSPECTION FORM

Jamison!
PROPERTY MANAGEMENT

Property/Location _____ Inspection Date _____

Instructions: Please mark each item for its existing condition.

| EXTERIOR | EXISTING CONDITION | | REMARKS |
	Good condition	Needs attention	if item needs attention
Foundation			
Walls			
Roof			
Electric Fixtures			
Windows/Screen			
Doors			
Gutters			
Shutters			
Mailbox			
Porch Deck			
GROUNDS			
Lawn			
Shrubs/Trees			
Walks			
Driveway			
Fence			
Exterior Storage			
SYSTEMS			
Cooling			
Heating			
Electrical			
Plumbing			
Security			
Water softener			
Sump Pump			
Garage door			
Water heater			
Lawn sprinkler			
LIVING ROOM			
Floor			
Walls			
Ceiling			
Electric fixtures			
Windows			
Doors/Locks			
Closet			

Page 1 of 3

North Carolina Association of REALTORS®, Inc.

STANDARD FORM 415
Revised 7/2002
© 7/2002
Move in

Tenant Initials _____ Landlord Agent Initials _____

Jamison Realty - Keller Williams RP, 110 Matthews Station Street, Suite (D Matthews, NC 28105
Paul Jamison

Phone: 704-846-3663   Fax: 704-847-3663   www.ziplogix.com

Produced with zipForm® by zipLogix 18070 Fifteen Mile Road, Fraser, Michigan 48026.

FORM 415
Revised 7/2002
© 7/2016
Move in

Routine Inspection

Inspection Date: 00/00/0000
Property: 1234, City, State 12345
Current Tenant: Tenant | 123-456-7890
Page 1 of 3

Kitchen

	OK	Needs Follow Up
Refrigerator		
Sink		
Oven/Stove		
Cabinets		
Countertops		
Floors/Ceilings		
Walls		

Living Room

Windows		
Doors		
Floors/Ceilings		
Walls/Floors		

Bedroom

Windows		
Doors		
Floors/Ceilings		
Walls/Floors		

Bathroom

Sink		
Toilet		
Shower/Tub		
Floors/Ceilings		
Walls		

Potential Rent

Season	# Weeks	Rate/ Week	Total	Expenses Charged to Guest*
Spring	8	$1,500	$12,000	$600
Summer	12	$2,000	$24,000	$1,000
Fall	8	$1,500	$12,000	$600
Winter	5	$1,000	$5,000	$300
Total Annual Income Potential	**33**		**$53,000**	**$2,500**

* Sales tax, parking fees, bicycle rentals, cleaning fees, and so forth

Expenses

Insurance	$1,500
Maintenance	$2,500
Maintenance Reserves	$2,500
Mortgage Payment P&I	$24,000
HOA Fees	$6,000
Property Taxes	$3,000
Cleaning	$3,000
Management Fees	$8,200
Replacing Broken/Misplaced Items	$1,000
Marketing	$1,000
Total Expenses	**$52,700**

VACATION RENTAL CONTRACT

Jamison!
PROPERTY MANAGEMENT

123 Ocean Boulevard, Resort Town, SC 29926 – Rental Agreement

Date: May 5, 2019

Name: Jenny Doe
Address: 321 Landlocked Drive, Charlotte, NC 28202
Email: jennydoe28202@gmail.com
Phone: 704-867-5309

Please find the written confirmation for the rental of 123 Ocean Boulevard, Resort Town, SC 29926

Arrival Date: 8.4.18   (after 4:00pm)
Departure Date: 8.11.18   (before 10:00am)

Rent Due $3,385.78 rate (11% sales tax included) and $59 insurance policy plus $300 refundable pet deposit – (2) Amenity Cards –
Rental Required to hold property $3,358.78
Even though you paid insurance or a deposit, you are responsible for any additional damage.
If you need to purchase amenity cards, they are $35-$50 based on time of year/person (over 12 yrs old)/week. These cards must be paid for before you arrive and must be included in your final payment.

Damage Insurance
There is a $59 non-refundable damage insurance policy. Please remit with your final payment. The home will be inspected promptly after you check-out. If no damage has occurred, no dirty dishes sitting in the sink, a load of laundry has been started, no damage will be charged. If you leave dirty dishes and fail to start a load of laundry, you will be charged $75. This agreement does not limit the renter's liability for damages to $1,500. By signing this agreement, renters agree to be financially responsible for all damages, theft, and excessive cleaning, as well as all legal fees incurred by owner, as a result of litigation to collect for damages. Please call the owner if you accidentally break something or if you find something missing, so that we can have it replaced as soon as possible.

I certify that I as the renting party am at least 25 years of age.

Guest Signature: _____   Date: _____

All contracts should be sent to **Jamison Property Management, 500 W John St, Matthews, NC 28105**. A copy of this fully executed rental agreement will be returned to the Guest upon receipt of Guest's deposit, and final acceptance of same by Owner.

PETS: IF THEY CAUSE ANY DAMAGE, RENTER IS FULLY RESPONSIBLE. PLEASE FOLLOW PET POLICY. NO PETS ON FURNISHINGS, NOT TO BE LEFT ON SCREEN PORCH OR UNATTENDED TO WANDER HOME. IF YOU OR YOUR PET CAUSE DAMAGE, BE HONEST ENOUGH TO REPORT IT AND PAY TO FIX IT. NO CATS, NO EXCEPTIONS!

Cancellation and Hurricane Policies
A full refund is granted for a cancellation 90 days before arrival. A 2/3 refund is given for a cancellation between 60 and 90 days of arrival. A 1/3 refund is granted for cancellations between 30 and 60 days before arrival except during March through September, that is non refundable. There will be no refunds for cancellations made less than 30 days prior to arrival at any time. However, if we can re-rent your rental period, all monies will be refunded less a $100 processing fee.

While hurricanes can hit the Atlantic seacoast, history has shown it is rare when they come ashore at Fripp. However, we do not provide refunds for hurricanes or other weather related events. There are numerous insurance companies that provide this type of coverage.

_____ Renter's Initials

General Information
CHECK-IN IS 4:00PM, not before. CHECKOUT IS 10:00AM SHARP. A $50 late checkout fee will be charged if you stay beyond the 10:00 checkout time. Arrival on the island before the 4:00 check-in time is fine. You just will not be able to get into the house until 4:00. I'm sure you understand our desire to provide you with a clean house for your stay. Upon arrival, stop at the Security gate to pick-up your vehicle pass. All vehicles must have a pass. You can pick up your amenity cards and hit the beach anytime the day of your arrival. Remember to bring your own long distance prepaid phone card, we do not provide free long distance . If you bring your pet and you have not received written permission, **You will be asked to vacate the home**. RENTER WILL BE BRINGING A PET x__ YES   ____NO. Only 1 if approved.

It is against the law to block the bike path that runs in front of the house. Make sure your vehicle is not blocking the path. If you have extra vehicles, they can be parked at the Ocean Creek Golf Course parking lot. Car passes must be visible.

Garbage pickup days are listed on the refrigerator (Wed and Sat). [If a holiday falls on a garbage pick up day, (Memorial, Labor, Thanksgiving Day, etc) they will pick up the day after these holidays.] It is your responsibility to place the garbage bin on the

[... Policy and your Garbage responsibilities including Cancellation and Hurricane ...ng the cost of the time it takes to remedy by owner. ...your rental and we know you will enjoy your stay.] [sections of this agreement including Cancellation and Hurricane ...and agree with and will pay for any and all]

Place household garbage in large cinching your deposit if the garbage cans are EXCEPTIONS (The raccoons will loot not jeopardize your insurance. Take urged for it.

away from the house. Please do not throw find butts, we will file a claim.

...cy during non-business hours, call the ...mber where to reach you, and a brief ...hanical systems. Environmental stress ...ppliance or HVAC failure. If you ...e patient while we work to solve your ...es a year to prevent unexpected

...ring you the use of our golf carts as ...ompletely responsible for any ...Jamison or AV8TOR Sportswear, ...it.

...le for any and all damage to the ...eration of the golf carts for any ...he golf cart including and not ...cart. Fripp Island Security will

...cart, always turn the key off and ...the basket in the kitchen. The

...side (right side as you look at ...eat. The cart uses deep ...t will provide you plenty of ...the gas pumps. Again, the ...ing your stay, call us and ...ave two.

...n the garage, unplug the

Notes

ABOUT THE AUTHOR

Paul Jamison has had a passion for real estate since he was small. His mother always said that when he came inside the house after a long day outside, he brought half the real estate in the neighborhood stained on his clothes. So now you know that is how it got into his DNA and how it all began!

With twenty-seven years of advertising agency experience and thirty-four years since he bought his first investment property, Paul has grown a thriving real estate practice. His disciplines include residential, commercial, property management, and investment real estate in many areas of the country with his main focus primarily in the Carolinas. He has used his years of advertising and branding experience to help his clients learn, sell, and evaluate the creative side of the real estate market, where connecting to the buyers and sellers through a unique method of delivery brings stronger success and higher returns. Paul is also host of the weekly radio show *Your Real Estate Today.* The focus is to share information on market trends and shed light on the positive news and growth being involved in real estate has to offer. It's a live call-in format, so people call with questions for him and his special guests. You can listen to Paul's podcasts on Radio.com or WBT Charlotte talk radio on WBT.com.

Paul currently owns a portfolio of residential, commercial, and vacation properties that he and his team manage. Paul also manages a large portfolio of investment property for individual investors. The Jamison family of companies includes Jamison Realty, Jamison Property Management, and Jamison Property Investments. He and Kerry, his wife of twenty-nine years, share three sons and four grandchildren.

WHAT'S NEXT?

This book may reference some things that change over time, and each state or area may have different rules or philosophies. If you encounter such things or have questions, visit my website at **pauljamison.com** and send me your thoughts. I will create updates on a blog we can all enjoy. My website contact form sends emails directly to me, and the site will always be improving. Enjoy the journey. Enjoy making real estate a part of your success and financial plan.